POEMS &

POLITICAL

LETTERS OF

F. I. TYUTCHEV

POEMS &

POLITICAL

LETTERS OF

F. I. TYUTCHEV

Translated with

Introduction and Notes

by Jesse Zeldin

THE UNIVERSITY OF

TENNESSEE PRESS

KNOXVILLE

Library of Congress Cataloging in Publication Data

Tiutchev, Fedor Ivanovich, 1803–1873.
  Poems & political letters of F. I. Tyutchev.

    I. Zeldin, Jesse, 1923–   tr.   II. Title.
PG3361.T5A29 1973   891.7'1'3   73–4397
ISBN 0–87049–146–6

Preface

Following the common practice of modern Russian editions of Fyodor Tyutchev's works, I have divided the present translation into three parts: (1) the lyrical poems; (2) the political poems; and (3) the political letters. Each section is arranged in chronological order: the lyrical poems run from 1825, the probable year of the writing of "A Flash of Light," to 1873, the year of the writing of "A punishing God has deprived me of all," which was also the year of Tyutchev's death; the first of the political poems, "To Pushkin's 'Ode on Liberty,'" was probably written in 1820, although not printed until 1887, and the last, "Two Unities," was written in 1870; of the four political letters the first was written in 1844, the fourth in 1857. For the poems, all composed in Russian, I depended on the two-volume edition of K. V. Pigarev (Moscow: Izdatelstvo nauka, 1966); for the letters, all composed in French, I used the edition (the last one) of P. V. Bykov, St. Petersburg, 1913.

Although I have translated the vast majority of Tyutchev's poems, I omitted the poems he translated or adapted from poets of other languages than Russian (for example, Goethe, Heine, Byron, Michelangelo, Herder, Hugo, Racine, Shakespeare, Lamartine, Beranger); the poems he wrote in French; his very youthful poems (those written between 1816, when Tyutchev was thirteen years old, and 1820), all of which were either altogether unpublished during his lifetime or omitted from any collections of his work published during his lifetime; and those occasional poems which would be of little interest even to the specialist. Thus, out of some 300 original Russian poems of Tyutchev's, I have translated 220, as well as all 4 of his political letters.

The notes are intended for clarification of Tyutchev's subject matter where I felt such clarification was needed; the reader will therefore find more of them in connection with Tyutchev's political work than with his lyrics. All the political poems are thus dated in the notes, because of their references to contemporary events, and all the poems are dated in the index. Those poems I thought could stand alone I have left unannotated. I am deeply indebted to the Pigarev edition of the poems for many of the notes and the datings, although I must point out that I have not always agreed with Pigarev as to which poems are political and which lyric.

My main concern in these translations has been to translate, not to render, and certainly not to adapt. I have therefore avoided rhyme (Tyutchev always follows a rhyme scheme, although his rhymes are often far from pure), as I have avoided trying to follow the Russian meter (Tyutchev himself often mixes his meters, with a preference for iambic tetrameter), while at the same time I have tried to give some patterned rhythmical form to each of the poems. On the other hand, I have followed Tyutchev's stanzaic divisions strictly and have tried to indicate original line lengths wherever I could reasonably do so. In deference to contemporary taste, I have attempted to use modern English instead of reproducing Tyutchev's archaisms, old and rare words, made-up words, and negative adjectives. If the reader sometimes finds the syntax equivocal, it is so in the original. In any event, I have always remained conscious that poems are, after all, poems, not prose; it is my hope that some of the poetic quality of Tyutchev's work comes through.

It must be admitted, however, that not all of Tyutchev's poems are of the first rank. Few would disagree with Richard A. Gregg's statement that most of the political poems " . . . are vastly inferior to the rest of his verse."[1] Indeed, Gregg cites many authorities, from I. S. Aksakov to V. Gippius, in support of the view that Tyutchev's political poetry is "bad political verse."[2] While I do not agree entirely, still, in recognition of the situation, I have not tried to make any of the poems better—as a poem—than it is in the original (nor, of course, have I deliberately tried to make any worse). I also thought it

[1] Richard A. Gregg, *Fedor Tiutchev: The Evolution of a Poet* (New York and London, 1965), 141.
[2] *Ibid.*, 142.

viii

best to leave the ambiguities instead of trying to clarify them, a fault many translators commit.

In the long run, my purpose has been not so much to present Tyutchev as an artistic phenomenon, that is, as a "poet," high as his eminence may be, as to give the reader of English a chance to become acquainted with a spirit which is in many ways typical in nineteenth-century Russia, and which also bears many resemblances to attitudes prevalent in the Soviet Union today. It is therefore my hope that the reader will peruse Tyutchev's work *as a whole* rather than pick out a poem here or a prose passage there. For the purposes I had in mind it is the ensemble that counts much more than specific individual parts. And for further material on Tyutchev, the interested reader is referred to the bibliography furnished by Richard A. Gregg in *Fedor Tiutchev: The Evolution of a Poet.*

I should like to express my appreciation to the American Philosophical Society and to the Hollins College Ford Foundation Fund for the generous financial aid accorded me in the pursuit of this work. My thanks are also due to President John A. Logan, Jr., and the Board of Trustees of Hollins College for the sabbatical leave during which the greater part of this task was accomplished and to the Hollins College Travel and Research Fund for helping me to obtain many of the necessary research materials. Of particular aid was the work done by Miss Gigi McGuire in compiling bibliographies, running down out-of-print sources, and serving as a general factotum during the early stages of my endeavor.

JESSE ZELDIN

Sebasco Estates, Maine
August, 1973

Contents

POEMS &

POLITICAL

LETTERS OF

F. I. TYUTCHEV

Introduction

Fyodor Ivanovich Tyutchev is generally acknowledged to be one of Russia's finest lyric poets. Father Georges Florovsky, the dean of contemporary Slavists, once went so far as to write, "For the power and force of his aesthetic and philosophic conceptions, Tyutchev must be hailed as first among Russian poets,"[1] ahead even of Pushkin. Afanasy Fet, Tyutchev's greatest lyric rival, writing in 1859, five years after the appearance of the first collection of Tyutchev's poems, remarked, "Two years ago, on a quiet spring night, I was in the . . . Colosseum . . . looking up at a star-filled sky. . . . I saw only a small part of the sky, but I felt that it was vast and that there was no end to its beauty. It is with similar sensations that I read Tyutchev's lines."[2] Boris Pasternak is reported to have said that he owed more to Tyutchev than to any other Russian poet, probably in reference to Tyutchev's nature poems. The list of appreciations—if not to say encomia —could be greatly prolonged, especially if one were to take into account the statements of the Russian Symbolist poets, who saw Tyutchev as their most important predecessor.

Much less note has been taken of Tyutchev's political work, both in poetry and in prose, in spite of its obvious importance historically and in our own time, more, I suspect, because of disagreement with Tyutchev's point of view than because of serious evaluation of what he had to say. Indeed, many commentators have indulged in the schizophrenic school of criticism on this score,[3] as though the writer of the lyrics and the political poetry and prose was essentially two different people, the former a great art-for-art's-sake poet and the latter a second- or third-rate propagandist who either was not very bright or whose sentiments were grossly misplaced. Florovsky is one of the few to have recognized Tyutchev's importance intellectually as well as poetically, although he seems to me to go too far in his interpretation of Tyutchev as an Orthodox theocrat.

---

[1] "The Historical Premonitions of Tyutchev," *Slavonic Review* (III, Dec., 1924), 337.

[2] "O stikhotvoreniyakh F. Tyutcheva," *Russkoe Slovo*, No. 2 (1859), 67–68.

[3] This seems to be a risk among critics of Russian literature. Gogol, Dostoevsky, and Tolstoy, as examples, are all usually considered to have had crises which split their work in two. In the cases of Gogol and Tolstoy, the best work is considered to have been written before the change; in the case of Dostoevsky, after.

What Tyutchev would have thought of all this is difficult
to ascertain, although it is quite clear that he took his political
work very seriously and he had every reason—given the
attention paid him by such contemporaries as Chaadayev,
Khomiakov, Turgenev, and the Kireyevsky brothers—to
think his ideas worthy of attention. From the literary point
of view, he himself wrote no articles concerned with literary
criticism, very few poems on the subject of poetry,[4] and his
letters contain only scattered remarks on literature, although
they are full of political observations. If one were to take
all his writings into consideration—particularly his many
letters to his second wife—one could only reach the conclusion
that, unlike his commentators and some of his contemporaries,[5]
he did indeed think of himself more as an intellectual than
as an "artist," even though it was in his time that Pushkin
had established literature as a profession in Russia[6] and he
had every right to rate his poetry very high from the artistic
point of view. On the other hand, it is also true that in
Tyutchev's lifetime poetry was giving way to prose as the
popular medium of expression in Russia, to be revived only
at the turn of the century by the Symbolists, who discovered
in Tyutchev the philosophic base for a poetic renaissance.
In other words, Tyutchev may well have regarded literature,
particularly the writing of lyric poems, more as an avocation
—or as a means of private expression—than as a worthy
occupation in itself. Certainly, his indifference in regard to
the publication of collected editions of his poetry[7] seems to
support this point of view. His remark in the essay "Russia and
Germany," that he was completely indifferent to publicity,[8]
may be taken quite seriously as far as his lyric production
is concerned, although with great reservation as far as his
political work is concerned.

---

[4] See below, "You raised him in the great world's circle," "January 29,
1837," "Trust not, trust not the poet, maid," "Poetry," "In Memory of V. A.
Zhukovsky."

[5] Fet, Turgenev, and Nekrasov, for example.

[6] See André Meynieux, *Pouchkine, homme de lettres et la littérature profession-
nelle en Russie* (Paris, 1966).

[7] Turgenev supposedly revised some of Tyutchev's poems when he prepared 111 of them for the first collected edition of 1854, and Tyutchev showed
almost no interest in the matter (Gregg, *Fedor Tiutchev*, 20).

[8] See below, p. 159.

Like most of the Russian writers of the nineteenth century, Fyodor Tyutchev was heir to an upper-class background, to a noble background. He was born to a settled landowning and military family at Ovstug, near Bryansk, in 1803,[9] just four years after the birth of his great contemporary Pushkin. The family spent its winters, however, in Moscow, the old capital which was in later years to become the Slavophile center, as St. Petersburg was the center for the Westernizers. Indeed, the Tyutchev family was in Moscow at the time of the Napoleonic invasion of 1812 and had to leave to seek refuge in Yaroslavl. The memory of Napoleon was never to leave Tyutchev's thoughts.

The future poet's and thinker's education followed the usual path of private tutors and classical studies (mostly conducted in French, in which he received excellent training). He was most fortunate in that his tutors were genuinely interested in literary matters[10] and did their utmost to encourage his early poetic attempts. Certainly Tyutchev was well prepared when he left home in 1817 to attend the University of Moscow. He did well at the university (he took his final examinations in 1821), but more important perhaps than his studies was his circle of friends, almost all of whom were of a conservative and nationalistic turn of mind.[11]

Shortly after leaving the university, Tyutchev entered government service in the Ministry of Foreign Affairs, probably through the influence of his relative, Count A. I. Ostermann-Tolstoy, a believer in Orthodox unity who opposed what he thought of as the government's Western oriented foreign policy. In the spring of 1822, Tyutchev was posted to the Russian legation at Munich in Ostermann-

[9] For Tyutchev's biography I am mainly indebted to the first chapter of Gregg's book, to K. V. Pigarev, *Zhizn' i tvorchestvo Tyutcheva*, (Moscow, 1962), and to D. Strémooukhoff, "Introduction biographique," *La Poésie et l'idéologie de Tiouttchev* (Paris, 1937).

[10] One of these was S. E. Raich, a poet in his own right, who translated Virgil, Ariosto, and Tasso into Russian. Raich later edited the journal *Galatea*, in which he published some of Tyutchev's poems. Another was Merzlyakov, professor at the University of Moscow, who surrounded himself with young *littérateurs*. Merzlyakov's views, like Raich's, were largely classical.

[11] Among them were M. P. Pogodin and S. P. Shevyrev, both of whom later became leading Russian nationalist critics.

Tolstoy's train. He was to remain abroad for the next twenty-two years, as an official of the legation at Munich until 1837, with the Russian legation at Turin from 1837 to 1839, and in Munich in a private capacity from 1839 to 1844.

Tyutchev seems to have been of some success as a diplomat, since he received several promotions and eventually became chargé d'affaires, but these years abroad were of greater importance to him intellectually, politically, poetically,[12] and personally. Intellectually, it was in these years that he became acquainted with German romanticism and German philosophy, for Munich, then ruled by Louis I of Bavaria, was the brightest center of German culture. Tyutchev formed a personal friendship with Heine, engaged in discussions with Schelling, and was the first to translate Goethe into Russian. At the same time he became acquainted with Russian intellectuals passing through Munich, such as the brothers Kireyevsky, who were to become leaders in the Slavophile movement, and Prince P. A. Vyazemsky, who was to be one of the more important nineteenth-century Russian poets.[13] Politically, he found himself in an advantageous position to observe developments in the West and to take note of Western attitudes towards Russia. Poetically, Tyutchev's contact with Western poets seems to have confirmed him in his avocation and defined the lyric direction of his talent. Personally, it was in these years that he contracted both his marriages, both to widows of German background: first, in 1826, to Elizabeth Peterson, four years older than the diplomat, widow of the Russian minister at Weimar, and mother of three children; then, in 1839, one year after Elizabeth's death, to Ernestine Dörnberg, who was well on the way to bearing Tyutchev's child at the time of the marriage (he had met her in 1833 and his marriage was probably the reason for his leaving the Foreign Service in 1839, since he took French leave at the time). He was to enter into one more love alliance that we are sure of, that with Elena Alexandrovna Deniseva, who was some twenty-three years younger than he; the affair continued

[12] Ettore lo Gatto, for example, considers that Tyutchev's best poems were written between 1830 and 1840 (*Histoire de la littérature Russe*, translated from the Italian by M. and A. M. Cabrini [Paris, 1965], 184). In this volume the first of these poems is "Just as ocean encircles the globe of earth," the last "Trust not, trust not the poet, maid."

[13] See below, "On the Jubilee of Prince Peter Andreyevich Vyazemsky."

for fourteen years, from 1850 until Deniseva died in 1864, after having given Tyutchev three children. It was Deniseva who inspired most of Tyutchev's love poetry, although he always retained strong attachments to the other women with whom he had been involved.

It was also in these years that Tyutchev began to publish some of his work. In 1836, Prince I. S. Gagarin, a member of the Russian Legation in Munich at the time and a man well known in Russian intellectual circles, took some of Tyutchev's poems to Russia. There he showed them to Zhukovsky, Vyazemsky, and Pushkin, the last of whom printed them in his journal *The Contemporary*. Tyutchev was to continue journal publication throughout his poetic career.

By the time he returned to Russia in 1844, to reside there until his death in 1873 (although he took many trips abroad in the interim), Tyutchev's intellectual and poetic conceptions had reached maturity and were not to change, despite the increasing personal pessimism we can discern in his work as time goes on. His political interests never lost their strength, and he continued virulently to express his Slavophile and pan-Slavic convictions until the end of his life. Certainly, the government of Russia saw no reason not to place its trust in him, for in 1848 he was appointed senior censor in the Russian Ministry of Foreign Affairs and in 1858 he was named president of the Committee of Foreign Censorship. During these years he became known as one of the wittiest *mondains* in Russia and formed a large circle of friends and acquaintances among the brightest lights of Russian culture of the time.

Clearly, there is little in Tyutchev's external life to excite the commentator who looks for drama. In the absence of such drama, critics have turned to his internal life and, basing themselves on Freud, have resorted to paradox. Gregg, for example, describes Tyutchev as follows:

> The Slavophile who could not stand life in Russia; the enemy of the West who pined to return there; the inveterate *mondain* who found St. Petersburg society perverted; the theocrat who lived without faith—these paradoxes can, it would seem, be multiplied almost at will. And running parallel to them are the contradictions inherent in his poetry: nature is an animate, meaningful whole—nature is a sphinx without a riddle; God exists and His truth is plain to all—there is no God; chaos attracts the poet—chaos repels him; Russia's essence is her profound

Christian humility—Russia's military might will extend her borders from the Nile to the Elbe.[14]

As Gregg points out, many critics have attempted to deal with these "paradoxes" (which can, in Gregg's own words, "be multiplied almost at will") by adopting a philosophical approach which at best, Gregg believes, distorts Tyutchev by suppressing the contradictions.[15] Gregg, on the other hand, working with what he believes are the "truths" of Freudianism, rejects the philosophic approach and adopts psychoanalysis: it is " . . . precisely the troubled and paradox-ridden self which informed his entire *oeuvre*."[16]

The first important critical acceptance of Tyutchev, however, in the article by the poet and editor N. A. Nekrasov, "Minor Russian Poets," which appeared in *The Contemporary* in January 1850, praised Tyutchev's lyrical poetry not for its philosophic content or self-revelation, but for the vividness of his descriptions of nature. "The great value of Tyutchev's poems," said Nekrasov, "lies in the vivid, graceful, and plastic painting of nature. . . . There is no doubt that the most difficult poetic style is that of poems apparently without subject, without thoughts; here we have a landscape in verse, a little picture marked by two or three strokes thanks to which the picture as a whole takes shape in the reader's imagination."[17] The novelist Ivan Turgenev did not go so far as Nekrasov, but he too emphasized the impression of the poems: " . . . each of his poems began with a thought, but a thought . . . which burst into flame under the influence of a profound feeling or a strong impression."[18] Later, when Tyutchev was adopted by the Russian Symbolists as their precursor, great emphasis was placed upon his individualism and his non-worldliness (in contrast to Nekrasov), his use, one might say, of nature as an "objective correlative," as a set of symbols for a higher reality (this is, of course, the approach of Vladimir Solovyov, the philosopher and mystic, in his 1895 article on Tyutchev, which may be regarded as

[14] Gregg, *Fedor Tiutchev*, 23–24.
[15] *Ibid.*, 24–25.
[16] *Ibid.*, 26.
[17] Cited by Charles Corbet in *Nekrasov, l'homme et le poète* (Paris, 1948), 144.
[18] "Neskol'ko slov o stikhotvorenniyakh F. I. Tyutcheva," in *Polnoe sobraniye sochinenii* (Moscow, 1963), V, 426.

the first step towards Tyutchev's resurrection).[19] This carries
the corollary that Tyutchev was a poet interested in art for
art's sake, in contrast to the "social" poets. In this view, he
comes close to being a mystic whose art is especially congenial
to the moderns'. He becomes, indeed, a "poet's poet."

On the other hand, Tyutchev, unlike the Symbolists, seems
to have reached a certain stage of popularity in the Soviet
Union today (with the exception of the political articles,
which have not been reprinted since 1913).[20] Pigarev's remarks
on this subject[21] are worth quoting at length:

> A new stage both in the study of Tyutchev and in genuine
> popularization of his poetry opened after the Great October
> Socialist Revolution.
>
> It is well known that V. I. Lenin loved Tyutchev's poetry.
> . . . Tyutchev's name was included in the list of writers' names
> inscribed in the 1918 edict on so-called "monumental propa-
> ganda" signed by Lenin. In 1920 a museum named for the poet
> opened on what used to be the Tyutchev landed estate Muranovo
> outside Moscow.
>
> In the Soviet era Tyutchev has finally ceased to be a poet "for
> the few" initiated into the "mysteries" of poetry. Every new
> edition of Tyutchev's poetry in no matter how many copies,
> does not long remain on bookstore shelves, which is the best
> evidence of reader demand for his verses.
>
> After October Tyutchevian texts which were unknown earlier
> were discovered and published, among them the epigrammatic
> epitaph to Nicholas I,[22] the series of translations from Goethe,
> Heine, and others. The first studies of the archival materials shed
> light on the creative "laboratory" of the poet and on his per-
> sonality as a man.
>
> In his lines "On Tyutchev's little book of poetry," Fet once
> asserted, "Tyutchev will never be popular." But Tyutchev has
> become popular, and not only because his best verses have been
> translated into regional dialects and into other languages of our
> multinational country. Tyutchev has become popular above

[19] "Poeziya F. I. Tyutcheva," *Vestnik Evropy*, II (1895), 736–52.

[20] There have been some six separate editions of Tyutchev's poetry in
the Soviet period: two by G. I. Chulkov, in 1933 and 1935; one by Pigarev
and V. Gippius in 1939; two by Pigarev alone, in 1957 and 1966; and one
of the poems and letters of Tyutchev by Pigarev in 1957. There have also
been some eighteen articles and six books devoted to Tyutchev individually
in this period.

[21] "Poeticheskoe naslediye Tyutcheva," in *F. I. Tyutchev: Lirika* (Moscow,
1966), I, 312–14.

[22] See below, p. 138

all because our Russian language and Russian poetry became popular along with the new socialist culture.

Never has the name of Tyutchev, citations from his verses—either direct or paraphrased—and epigraphs borrowed from him been encountered so often as now in the pages of our newspapers and magazines. All this testifies to the fact that Tyutchev is entering more and more deeply not only into the consciousness of Soviet poets and prose-writers, but also into the consciousness of the Soviet reader. The circle of Tyutchev scholars, which not long ago was limited to a few names, is widening. In the newest works on him, which appraise his creative work as one of the most important and original phenomena of Russian literature, the epithets "genius" and "great" are unreservedly awarded to Tyutchev the poet.

Pigarev's statements—aside from the assertion of Soviet continuity with Russia's past—are most interesting in that they indicate a return to the Nekrasovian view of Tyutchev as a painter in words,[23] that is, a return to a basically appreciative attitude and a rejection of both the philosophic and the psychological approaches, to the neglect, however, of Tyutchev's prose and of his political poetry.[24] The most recent Soviet commentators thus continue the distinction made by their earliest pre-Soviet precursors.

However, all the interpretations of Tyutchev's work thus far referred to in reality consider but one part of it, the lyric, which admittedly forms by far the major part of his output. But Tyutchev did have a point of view, and it seems to me at least possible that his point of view, like that of most men, was consistent, that there is a principle underlying his work which does make it of a piece. After all, he did have a brain; indeed, as we know, his intellect was much valued by some of the brightest men of his time. And no one would quarrel, I think, with the proposition that his mind was largely influenced by the dominant trend of the early nineteenth century, romanticism.

It must also be recognized, however, that romanticism was not a unified movement, although it did have a single base. That base, in revolt against the Renaissance, was a conviction

---

[23] Nekrasov is officially very highly regarded in the Soviet Union.

[24] Thus, Pigarev relegates the political poems to vol. 2 of the 1966 edition. "Of course," he says, "all these verses should have a place in a complete collection, but that place should be a subordinate one in relation to the 'golden treasury' of Tyutchev's lyrics." (*F. I. Tyutchev*, 316.)

of the unity of the universe, which all romantics thought to
be good. Their work is imbued with the celebration of the
"all" rather than of the "thises and thats," of mankind rather
than of men. This conviction could lead to the pantheism
of a Wordsworth (there are traces of such a pantheism in
Tyutchev) and to the rational World-Spirit of a Hegel; it
could lead to the all-embracing egoism of a Byron, the
platonism of a Shelley, the Rights of Man of the French
Revolution, the *sobornost'* of Khomiakov, to radical nihilism,
and to the ethnic celebrations of our time. All saw the world
as good (in some cases "doing what comes naturally" is
almost a fetish), as the good "one," but as either having
been disrupted by individual human blindness or in danger
of such disruption. The Westerners who saw it in the former
way became enchanted with the Middle Ages while they
retained a radicalism in political and social affairs (unlike the
Russians and Germans), a radicalism, however, which was
conceived more in terms of a return to Truth than in terms
of a new departure; those who saw it in the latter way took
the conservative path of historical legitimacy, in terms of
continuity rather than in terms of leaps, even "gradual leaps."
It is to this second group that Tyutchev belongs. For him
the principles of unity are already established, as they are
established for his most important teachers, the Germans.

He was quite well aware that in the political arena the
prime force in nineteenth-century Europe was the struggle
for national unity on the parts of the Germans and the Italians.
This struggle was also taking place in Russia, where the
desire for unity took the form of Slavophilism and then of
pan-Slavism (as in Germany it was pan-Germanism) and of
Orthodoxy (Russia is perhaps the last of the European nations
—if Russia is European—to take its official religion seriously,
unless we consider Marxism a religion). For Tyutchev, both
Slavic and Orthodox unity were in the process of being
factually achieved but in danger of being frustrated by the
forces of the Revolution, which in his lyric poems are the
forces of chaos.

Stylistically, in terms of literary attachment, of course,
Tyutchev never gave up his connections with the eighteenth
century. Much of his literary training had been in the
eighteenth-century classical—or pseudoclassical—school and
all through his life he retained certain characteristics of that
school: the use of archaisms, a certain rhetorical tone

(particularly in his political poems), a tendency to syllabic versification, and "composed" adjectives. Indeed, critic after critic has pointed out Tyutchev's connections with Derzhavin, the leading eighteenth-century Russian poet. His sympathies here, from the intellectual rather than from the stylistic point of view, reflect his attachment to what he considered a Russian continuity, to Slavism. The previous three hundred years of the West, that is, of the Renaissance, he saw as an attempt to destroy the Truth. His objections to the West all refer to what he thinks of as the revolutionary West, the West of the schism, of the Reformation, of 1789, 1830, and 1848.

It is quite clear that much of Tyutchev's attitude had its root in fear, for he was only too well aware of forces in himself that corresponded to those at work on the world stage. As so much of his poetry shows, he was deeply conscious of his own egoistic attachment to the material world; he, as he put it, the "lord of earth, stuck fast to earth." Over and over again he speaks of his desire to escape his ego, to escape from time and be a part of the all. The ego for him was the individual impulse that corresponded to the Revolution, to chaos, to the abyss. It is the disruptive power that results in fragmentation; it destroys harmony, replacing unity with anarchy. It is the jangling discordant note in the universal chord. In one of his poems, for example, he says:

> There is a melody in sea waves,
> A concord in elements' quarrels,
> And a mellifluous musical rustling
> Runs streaming in rippling rushes.
>
> There is a steady system in all,
> Full consonance in nature;
> It is only in our phantom freedom
> That we sense discord with her.
>
> Whence and how has discord arisen?
> Why does the soul not sing
> In choir with the sea, why does
> This thinking reed complain?

The same idea is also expressed in his more famous "Silentium":

> Be silent, be secret, hide
> Your feelings and your dreams.
> Deep in the depths of your soul
> Let them mutely rise and set,

As clear stars do in the night:
Admire them and be silent.

How does a heart speak out?
How explain yourself to another?
Will he grasp what you live by?
Pronounced thought is a lie.
Your burrowing troubles the waters:
Drink of them and be silent.

Know how to live within—
Your soul contains a world
Of mysterious, magical thoughts;
The outer tumult stifles,
The beams of daylight blind:
Hear their song and be silent.

It is clear in these poems that unity is a fact already existent and that thought, the rational, the "thinking reed," as Pascal called man long before Tyutchev used the phrase, is destructive of that unity. It is not man's task to analyze reality; it is his task simply to be aware of it and to live in it. "Hear their song and be silent."

In unity and harmony, further, is life itself; it is the very salvation of man, guarding him against the horrors of the abyss which yawns always ready to engulf and destroy him, the abyss which is the night of the soul. In "Day and Night" Tyutchev says:

The lofty will of the gods has granted
That over the secret world of spirits,
Above th'anonymous abyss,
A gold-brocaded cloak be spread.
Day is this resplendent cloak,
Day, of earth-born the reviver,
The healer of deep suffering souls,
The friend of men and deities.

But day is fading; night has come;
It has arrived; the fated world's
Bliss-giving, sheltering cloak is rent
And cast away. Th'abyss is bared
To us in all its horror and gloom,
No barrier now is there between us—
And that is why night frightens us so.

One might say that in Tyutchev's view the harmonious universe of which man is properly a part is the legitimate universe, indeed, the sanctified universe. Thus, to live in this universe is equivalent to living in God's world. It is the world of which Dostoevsky's Father Zosima was speaking when he said that this earth is already Paradise, if we would only see it. Unfortunately, there are lost souls in this world who do not see it. Of such persons he wrote:

> They do not see and do not hear,
> They live in darkness while in this world,
> They never feel the breath of the sun,
> Nor know of life in the waves of the sea.
>
> Light has not entered into their souls,
> Spring has not flowered in their breasts,
> Woods have not spoken in their presence,
> And the starry night is dumb to them.
> . . . .
> Not theirs the fault: let a deaf-mute catch
> If he can the life of organ tones.
> Alas! not even a mother's voice
> Can rouse concern within his soul.

As he put it elsewhere, it is the deceits of the senses that tend to separate us from the Truth. The concord of the universe is to be perceived, not sensed. Secularism and materialism, Tyutchev was convinced, frustrated this perception, removed the person from the harmony, and thus resulted in discord. A discordant universe is both false and evil (one is again reminded of Father Zosima). It is the angels in Heaven who make the music of the spheres, not the followers of Satan in Hell. In lyric poem after lyric poem, Tyutchev speaks of this harmony, of the rhythm of the universe, of the concordant unity of all existence. Here is peace and salvation, for here is the world of God. Tyutchev is not only a philosophic poet in his lyric poems; he is even more a religious poet singing the glory of God. Indeed, it is the musical quality of his verse—to which no English translation has thus far done full justice—which has most impressed his readers. And Tyutchev was himself aware of the necessity for music—that is, harmony—in poetry. He was quite specific on this subject in his poem entitled "Poetry":

> Amid the thunders, amid the fires,
> Amid the seething of our passions,
> In elemental flaming discord,
> From heaven she flies down to us,
> Heaven-sent to the sons of earth,
> An azure clarity in her gaze.

> And over the mutinous rioting sea
> She pours her reconciling oil.

Harmony, thus, is the proper state of the universe; whatever discord there may be comes from man. This applies not only to the natural world, however; it also applies to history. There is God-established "historical legitimacy," as he puts it in his essay on "Russia and Germany," and usurpation. He was convinced, at least up until the Franco-Prussian War of 1870, that every people had a right to its own unity, that such unity was, indeed, a Christian principle. Opposed to this principle is the revolutionary anti-Christian principle which venerates the individual ego and secular power. The Revolution is therefore illegitimate and anarchic. Tyutchev, the conservative, sees the struggle as one between the sanctified and established and the secular and egoistic, between good and evil. The same principle that pervades his lyric poetry informs his political work.

Russia, the successor, the continuer, of the true Christian Empire, brings together, in a kind of counterpoint, the world of human affairs and the world of God, infusing the former with the meaning of the latter, as Christ Himself did in the Incarnation. Hands had been laid upon Russia, so that it is in actuality the historically legitimate Empire. As he put it in an apostrophe to his nation,

> Crushed by the Cross's burden,
> The Heavenly Tsar has traveled
> In servile guise across you,
> My native land, with blessing.

Of course, Tyutchev's conviction of the holiness and legitimacy of Russia could lead to what a non-Russian mind might consider a frightening conclusion, as in Tyutchev's "Russian Geography":

> Moscow, Peter's city, and Constantine's city
> Are the holy capitals of the Russian realm.
> But where its outer limit, where its border,
> To north, to east, to south, and where the sun sets?
> Destiny will unmask them in future times.
>
> Seven inland seas, and seven great rivers—
> From Nile to Neva, from Elbe to China, from Volga
> To Euphrates, from the Ganges to the Danube—
> That is the Russian realm. And never will
> It pass, as the Spirit foresaw and Daniel predicted.

This legitimate realm, a choir of the spirit singing in harmonious unanimity, "the Europe of Peter the Great," stands face to face with "the Europe of Charlemagne," the Europe which has denied God in favor of secular power, the Europe of Rome and Revolution.[25]

In Tyutchev's mind there is no doubt but that Russia represents the principle of unity and it is Russia that has ceaselessly struggled to assert this unity, not only for herself but for all peoples. When Russia came into the Napoleonic Wars against France, he says in "Russia and Germany," she did so because

> she wanted once and for all to carry the day for the right, for historical legitimacy, over the revolutionary process. And why did she want to do that? Because the right, historical legitimacy, is her cause, her own cause, the cause of her future, it is the right that she demands for herself and for her own.

Thus, Russia supports German unity because unity is the principle itself of Russia, a unity Russia achieved with the expulsion of the Tatars and which western Europe still envies her.

It is in his essay "Russia and the Revolution," however, that Tyutchev comes more profoundly to grips with the problem. Russia and the Revolution are the only two real powers in the world, representing two entirely opposed principles which Tyutchev clearly defines:

> Russia is above all a Christian empire .... It is so by that faculty of renunciation and sacrifice which forms the basis of its moral nature. The Revolution is ... anti-Christian.
>
> The human ego which wants to depend only on itself, which neither recognizes nor accepts any other law than that of its own pleasure, the human ego, in short, which substitutes itself for God is certainly not something new among men; but what is new is this absolutism of the human ego exalted into a political and social right and with this claim aspiring to take over society. It is that new invention which in 1789 was called the French Revolution.

[25] One cannot resist mentioning a comparison with the late nineteenth-century American phrase "manifest destiny" and the slogan "Rum, Romanism, and Rebellion." A study of Russia, fortunately or unfortunately, always brings the United States to mind; the turn of romanticism to religion in both countries is particularly striking—we even find it today in the youthful "Jesus movement" in the United States, in the revival of religion in Russia, and in the more standard turns to Marxism and Maoism.

Tyutchev's view of Russia was not, of course, original. It was typical of the Slavophile attitude and of the romantic bias, whose culminating and most potent expression was Spengler, which conceived of the explanation of historical movements in terms of national *Geister* (if this makes Tolstoy a romantic, de Gaulle a romantic, the Québecois romantics, and Nasser a romantic, so much the better). For Tyutchev, Russia is, in a very profound sense, a conserver of Truth, not an aggressor but a humble witness of Christ. The aggressor in the struggle between Truth and Falsity is the Revolution. Tyutchev perhaps expresses this view best in his "Sea and Cliff":

> It rises rebelling and seethes,
> It slashes, whistles, and squalls,
> It would leap up to stars,
> Up to th'unshakable heights.
> Is it hell, has hellish power
> Laid out Gehenna's fire
> Beneath the seething cauldron,
> Has it reversed the deeps
> And set them upside down?
>
> With breakers of raging waves
> The sea rollers ceaselessly beat,
> With squall, whistle, scream, and howl,
> Against the coastal cliff.
> But calm and haughty, by whims
> Of waves remaining unmoved,
> Steadfast, immutable,
> Old as the universe,
> Our giant, still you stand!
>
> Enfrenzied by the battle,
> As though to final assault,
> The howling waves anew
> Swarm over your granite bulk.
> But its roaring onslaught broken
> By the immutable stone,
> The shattered billow splashed back,
> And the enfeebled gush
> Now streams a muddy foam.
>
> So stand, O mighty cliff!
> Wait but one hour, another—
> The rolling wave will weary
> Of battle with your heel.
> With its evil game fatiguing,
> It will subside anew.

And howling and battle over,
Beneath the giant's heel
The wave will stretch anew.

There are few statements which more clearly express the conservative attitude than this. It was, of course, written in 1848. Even more interestingly, it is included by Pigarev, in his 1966 two-volume edition of Tyutchev's poems, in volume one, the volume which contains what Pigarev regards as the best of Tyutchev's poems. Like so many of Tyutchev's political poems, it can, from the Soviet point of view, be read as a commentary on the contemporary situation.

For Tyutchev, however, Russia preserves not only the Christian principle of humility in opposition to the atheistic, secular principle of the ego; it also preserves the principle of unity against the forces of divisiveness. In practical terms, this means that Russia is the guardian of Slavic wholeness. Nationality is not simply a matter of geographic boundaries; it is ethnic. *Narod* means "people" as well as "nation," and so it did to Tyutchev. After all, the nearest equivalent to the term *narod* is the German *Volk*, a popular word among the German ideologists of Tyutchev's time (as it was a popular term in the 1930's) among whom he had lived and with whom he had conversed for over twenty years of his maturity. As so many in Germany yearned for the unity of the *Volk*, so Tyutchev yearned for the unity of the *narod*. It is out of this conservative romanticism that his pan-Slavism was born.

According to Tyutchev, the Slavs, who are in reality one, have been torn apart by anti-Christian forces: aliens from Asia, Magyars, Tatars, and Turks; and the Teutons of Europe (Germanic right to unity did not, in Tyutchev's mind, include rule over Slavs; it must also be remembered that Germany for him was west of the Elbe and north of the Alps and did *not* include Bohemia). The Slavs were one by blood, whole in spirit, with one champion—Russia. For the Slavic peoples to be united in political fact under the leadership of Russia was thus no more than to make manifest an already existent reality. Tyutchev, in this sense, did not wish to bring a new order of things into being; he wished only to preserve the unity that was already there.[26]

---

[26] In this connection, one cannot help but be reminded of the Comintern in Stalin's days; the principle of unity—of unanimity, indeed—was not only invoked but practiced. In many cases small changes in Tyutchev's terminology

Thus the suppression of the Polish revolt of 1831 took place, according to Tyutchev, as a sacrifice, much like Agamemnon's sacrifice of Iphigenia (for obvious reasons he chose to forget about Clytemnestra). Russia will keep Poland's ashes sacred and "Our common freedom, like the Phoenix, / Will be reborn in them." Slavic unity will at last be re-established, Tyutchev says in another poem, when Poland is reconciled with Russia. Significantly enough, this reconciliation will take place in Kiev and Constantinople, the ancient capitals of Slavdom and Orthodoxy. Poland, in short, is the brother fallen away who must be returned to the fold, much like Czechoslovakia in 1968.

Indeed, the Slavs in the center of Europe, the Czechs, were as important to Tyutchev as they later proved to be to the Soviets. As early as 1841, Tyutchev called upon the Czechs to reassert their unity with Russia in a kind of war of liberation. His poem to Hanka speaks of Hanka, whom Tyutchev had met in Prague, as a hero who "enkindled a beacon in darkness" with his affirmation of the oneness of the Slavic nature. Twenty-six years later, on the occasion of the Slavic Conference held in Petersburg and Moscow, he again called upon the now-dead Hanka and his vision of Slavdom. His poem "To the Slavs," read at the opening of the Conference in Petersburg, speaks of the Slavs as "a single people," "offspring of a single mother," "brothers born," called to unity. Finally, his second poem "To the Slavs," also written for the conference and read at a banquet on May 21, 1867, in response to the statement of Count von Beest, Austrian minister of foreign affairs at the time, that "*Man muss die Slaven an die Mauer drücken*,"[27] speaks of the home and defender that all Slavs have in the Russian Empire, which is once more compared to a granite cliff withstanding the onslaughts of the West.

Tyutchev's opposition to the West is precisely on the grounds that the West seeks to destroy the holy unity of Slavdom and the special mission of Russia. In "Great Day of Kiril's Death," he calls upon Russia in the following terms:

> Trust not in aliens, native land,
> Their wisdom false, their brazen fraud.
> Like holy Kiril, do not forsake
> Your glorious ministry to the Slavs.

---

would make him a quite fit representative of the conservatism that has ruled the Soviet Union for the past forty years (at least).

[27] "The Slavs must be pressed to the wall."

And in "Two Unities," written at the time of the Franco-Prussian War, Tyutchev summarized his position:

> Out of the cup o'erflowing with God's wrath
> Blood gushes across the land; the West is drowning.
> Blood gushes over you too, our friends and brothers.
> O Slavic world, more tightly close your ranks!
>
> "Our unity," our days' seer has proclaimed,
> "Can only be welded together of iron and blood."
> But we will try to weld it together of love—
> And we will see which one will last the longer.

The unity of Slavdom, as he often calls it, is for Tyutchev a reality based on blood kinship. The unity of Orthodoxy— for which read Christianity—is based on God and the One Church established by Him. In both cases the unity is legitimate, historically and religiously. God and the world, one may say, come together in terms of the legitimate establishment. In Russia and Orthodoxy the Truth is preserved against the separatist tides of revolutionary atheism and Roman desire for secular power. In Russia and Orthodoxy is preserved that legitimate authority whose task it is to struggle against the usurpations of Revolution and Rome. It is that authority's mission to keep the world from sliding into the abyss, to preserve harmony against discord, order against chaos. Tyutchev concludes his essay "Russia and the Revolution" as follows:

> And when has this mission been clearer and more obvious? It can be said that God writes it in letters of fire across a sky black with storms. The West is on its way, everything is collapsing, everything is being engulfed in a general conflagration, the Europe of Charlemagne as well as the Europe of the treaties of 1815; the Papacy of Rome and all the royalties of the West; Catholicism and Protestantism; the faith long lost and reason reduced to absurdity; order henceforth impossible, liberty henceforth impossible, and on all these ruins piled up by it, civilization committing suicide.
>
> And when over this huge wreck we see this Empire float larger than ever, like a Holy Ark, who will doubt her mission; is it for us, her children, to prove skeptical and faint-hearted?

All the difficulties are ultimately the fault of Rome, the "root of the western world." Although, as Tyutchev puts it in "The Roman Question," "Jesus Christ had said, 'My Kingdom is not of this world,'" still "Rome, after separating itself from the Oneness, believed it had the right, in an interest

Introduction

which it identified with the interest of Christianity itself, to
set up a Kingdom of Christ as a kingdom of this world."
Rome "did not deny the tradition, it was satisfied with confiscating it for its own advantage. But is not usurpation of the
divine the same as its denial?" Rome "ceased to be a society
of the faithful freely united in spirit and truth under the law
of Christ in the midst of the great human society. It became
an institution, a political power—a State within a State." By
this secularization, Rome gave rise to rivalries and conflicts,
to divisiveness, and thus "mortally wounded the very principle
of authority in the West." Rome, instead of preserving unity,
shattered it. Again, it is the claim to supremacy of the human
ego, anti-Christian in essence, that destroys authority, legitimacy, unity, Truth. Further, to submit to separateness means
to submit to the mortal and perishable, to death. It is to play
the part of Satan, a part played by Rome in the religious realm
and by Poland in the Slavic Realm.

Unity is thus for Tyutchev a principle of life itself, a religious
principle, inherent in the very nature of the universe that God
has established. Given this principle, Tyutchev's world view is
as much one as is Hegel's. More importantly, however, his
conservative romanticism is a part of the chain that links
together the Slavophiles, the pan-Slavists, and Dostoevsky
himself. Indeed, Prince Myshkin's famous anti-Roman speech
in The Idiot reads almost like a paraphrase of "The Roman
Question," as do many other passages in Dostoevsky which
deal with intellectual pride and the sin of overemphasis on the
individual human ego. It is the liberal, with his emphasis on
human reason, sacrificing vision to examination, who seeks
to destroy what has been sanctified by the Lord. "While,"
Tyutchev says to the liberal, "you may have instructed the
revolutionary principle as the Eternal did Satan to molest only
the body of Job without touching his soul, be well convinced
that the revolution, less scrupulous than the angel of darkness,
will take no notice of your injunctions." For Tyutchev, those
who applaud and further revolution are one with those who
cannot catch the "life of the organ tones." A true romantic,
he would have agreed, curiously enough, with the greatest of
the apostles of the ego, Byron, who, looking at the universe,
came to the conclusion that "only man is vile."

From the point of view of world-conception, there is no
question but that Tyutchev represents one aspect of the famous
Russian "search for national identity" of the nineteenth cen-

tury, a search the very foundation of which was a romantic outlook. For him Russian holiness, Russian right, passed beyond mere rational analysis, in spite of the attention he gives to political detail in his essays. In one of his poems, the most positive on this point that he ever wrote, he said:

> Not by the mind is Russia understood,
> Nor is she measured by a common rule:
> She has a special stature of her own;
> In Russia one can only put his faith.

What Tyutchev did not realize was that he, a conservative who believed in sanctification, a supporter of authority, order, and unity, one who had a vision of the oneness of all creation, was in fact far more a revolutionary, both intellectually and politically, than the so-called rationalists of the West whose rationalism was already on the decline, from Victor Hugo to Søren Kierkegaard. For Tyutchev was a romantic, and romanticism is the third of the great movements that has shaken the world since the fall of Rome. The first of these was the new unification movement of the Middle Ages, in both the West and the East, which accounts for the popularity of the Middle Ages among the romantics; the second was the Renaissance, a practical and individual realm which exalted personal accomplishment and examination, the age of heroes which laughed at teamwork, the world of which Shakespeare could say, "All order's gone," and of which John Donne felt compelled to say, "The new philosophy calls all in doubt," the world which witnessed the growth of Cartesian duality. The third is romanticism, the movement which calls again for unity, of both peoples and faith, from wars of liberation to establish ethnic rights to the "truths" of Marxism on the one hand, and of Freudianism, on the other. It is thus only in specifics that Tyutchev is peculiarly Russian, despite his connections with the Slavophiles (who are romantic enough in themselves). In general terms, all that matters to him is unity. It is not an accident that one of the results of romanticism, in political and social affairs as well as in sentiment and intellect, is greater and greater conformity, centralization, and ultimately totalitarianism. The oneness of all things finally results in the sameness of all men. In short, Tyutchev, in revolt against the Renaissance, as the Renaissance revolted against the Middle Ages, was on the winning side, in the broadest sense, for not only romanticism, but conservative romanticism gained the battle. The term *one world* would not be foreign to him at all, just as he would be likely to agree with the sentiments implied by "One small step for a man, one giant leap for mankind."

THE
LYRICAL
POEMS

A FLASH OF LIGHT ❧

Have you heard the subtle sound of the harp-box[1]
In the gloom-filled depths of the dark,
When a carefree midnight breeze disturbs
The sleep of the slumbering strings?

That sound now striking and startling, and then
Of a sudden fading away,
As though the climactic cry of torment
Evoked in them had been quenched.

As every zephyr's breath explodes
The sorrow in the strings,
You would say an angel's lyre is mourning
In the dust and across the skies.

O then our souls fly from this sphere
Of earth to a deathless one!
For we would press the friendly phantom
Of the past unto our breasts.

How lively is our faith, how happy
Our heart is, and how gay!
As though the ethereal stream of heaven
Were flowing through our veins.

But this is not our realm; in heaven
We soon would be wearied o'er.
It is not granted to paltry dust
To breathe the fire divine.

For no more than one burning moment
Will we break this magical dream,
Arise, and with troubled, trembling glance
Scan all the horizon round.

And then with heavy head, bedazzled
By this single flash alone,
Sink back anew, but not to calm;
Rather to wearying dreams.

---

[1] The "harp" was a kind of box with tautly stretched strings in it that vibrated musically when currents of air passed across them. It worked on the same principle as the Aeolian harp.

TO N.[2] 🦢

Your sweet gaze, with innocent passion flowing,
The golden dawn of your feelings divine,
Could not, alas, arouse their hearts to pity;
But serve it does as their silent reproach.

Those hearts in which the truth[3] does not reside
Flee from your loving, youthful gaze,
My friend, as they would flee from condemnation:
A childhood memory frightens them.

For me, however, this gaze is grace itself;
Your gaze lives in the depths of the soul
Like a spring of life, and it will live on in me:
I need it as the sky and breath.

Such blessèd spirits' sorrow is a beacon,
In the heavens alone it, heavenly, shines;
In the night of sin, in the depths of the awful abyss,
That pure fire will burn like a flame of hell.

SPRING STORM 🦢

I love a storm at May's beginning,
When spring's first thunderings,
As though in play and sportively,
Crash in the deep blue sky.[4]

Presaging peals are thundering,
Rain spatters and dust flies,
The threaded trail of pearl drops dropping
Turns golden in the sun.

Swift courses the torrent from the mountain,
Birds chatter in the woods.
The chatter in woods and mountainous clamor,
All gaily re-echo the thunder.

---

[2] The addressee of this poem is unknown.
[3] The word used here is *pravda*, which has connotations of justice as well as of truth.
[4] Literally, "When spring's first thunder, / As though frolicking and playing, / Crashes in the deep blue sky."

It is as though cup-bearing Hebe,
While feeding the eagle of Zeus,
Spilled laughing a thunder-boiling goblet
From heaven onto earth.

NAPOLEON'S TOMB[5] 𝕾🖎

Enlivened is nature with the advent of spring,
And everything glitters in this splendid season:[6]
The azure sky, the deep-blue sea,
The splendid sepulchre, and the cliff.
Fresh color has mantled the trees around,
And their shadows, in universal stillness,
Are barely rippled by the waft of the wave
Above the marble warmed by spring.

For long has Peroun[7] thundered his triumphs,
Their rumble resounds throughout the world.
. . . .
. . . .
Men's minds are filled by his great shade,
While his shade alone on this savage shore,
An alien, heeds the roar of the wave
And rejoices in the sea-birds crying.

CACHE–CACHE 𝕾🖎

Her harp is in its usual corner,
Carnations and roses at the window,
A midday sunbeam on the floor dozing:
A normal time. But where is she?

Who will help me find the prankish child?
O where, O where has my sylph disappeared?
I feel a magical closeness, as though
Divine Grace were flowing through all the air.

---

[5] At the time this poem was written, in 1828, Napoleon was still buried at St. Helena. His body was removed to Paris in 1840. See below, "Napoleon." Lines 11–12, now lost, were probably cut out by the censor.

[6] This line could also read, "And everything glitters in solemn quiet."

[7] Peroun is the ancient Russian god of thunder.

There is reason for the carnations' slyness,
There is reason, roses, for your leaves' blush
Intensifying and your scent's freshness:
I knew who was hidden, buried in blooms.

Did I not hear the sound of your harp?
Do you dream of hiding in the golden strings?
The metal shuddered when you stroked it,
And the sweet tremor has still not stilled.

How the anthers danced in the midday beams,
How vital the sparks in their natal fire!
I had looked into that flame before
And I knew well its ecstasy.

In a butterfly flew, and from bud to bud,
In seeming so carefree, began to flit.
Enough of your whirling, beloved guest!
Shall I not know you in your flight?

SUMMER EVENING 🐦

Already has earth slipped from its head
The incandescent globe of the sun,
And the wave of the sea engulfed
The peaceful fire of evening.

Bright stars have already mounted on high,
And with their dripping heads
Upraised the heavenly vault
Which weighed so heavy upon us.

A river most airy
Flows between heaven and earth,
My breast breathes easy and free,[8]
Relieved of sultriness.

A sweet throbbing has swept
Like a stream through nature's veins,
Like spring water lapping
Her burning legs.

[8] Literally, "more easily and more freely."

A VISION 🍂

> There is an hour in the night when all is still;
> At this hour of specters and miracles
> The living chariot of creation
> Resounding rolls in the sanctuary of the skies.
>
> And then night thickens, like chaos over the waters,
> Oblivion, like Atlas, oppresses dry land;
> And only the virginal soul of the Muse
> Do the gods arouse and call in prophetic dreams.

INSOMNIA 🍂

> Monotonous striking of hours—
> The wearisome tale of the night.
> Their language, like conscience, is foreign
> To all while heard by each.
>
> Has one of us griefless heard,
> Amid universal silence,
> The muted moans of time,
> The voice foretelling farewell?
>
> Ours is an orphaned world,
> Caught by unbending Fate,
> In our battle with all of nature
> Abandoned to ourselves.
>
> Our life is there before us,
> A phantom on the marge of earth:
> Like both our time and friends,
> It pales in distant twilight.
>
> A new, a young generation
> Meanwhile has bloomed in the sun,
> As we, our friends and time
> Pass on to be forgotten.
>
> A rare, metallic, funereal
> Voice performing a mournful
> Rite at the midnight hour
> Sometimes wails for us.

MORNING IN THE MOUNTAINS[9] ❧

> The celestial azure laughs,
> Washed by the storm of night,
> And the valley between the mountains
> Is waved by strips of dew.
>
> The mists veil only half
> The slopes of highest mountains,
> Which are like the airy ruins
> Of magic-created castles.

SNOW–CAPPED MOUNTAINS ❧

> Already the midday season
> Burns under vertical rays;
> The mountainside lies hidden
> By its black-screening forests.[10]
>
> Below, a mirror of steel,
> The liquid lakes gleam blue,
> And from rocks sparkling with heat
> Brooks haste to native depths.
>
> Meanwhile our valley world,
> Its strength all sapped and dozing,
> Sunk deep in languorous pleasure,
> Is immersed in midday mist.
>
> On the mountain the icy heights,
> Like a family of gods above
> Th' expiring earth, disport
> With the blue of the scorching sky.

TO N. N.[11] ❧

> You love and you know how to feign:
> When in a crowd my foot
> In secret touches yours,
> You answer me without a blush.

[9] This poem was originally printed, in 1830, as a whole with "Snow-Capped Mountains" under the general title of "Morning in the Mountains."

[10] "Screening" has been added to clarify Tyutchev's meaning in English.

[11] The addressee of this poem is unknown, but she is probably the same person as the subject of "To N.," above.

Unchanged is your absent, carefree mien,
Breasts' movement, glance, and smile.
While your husband, abhorréd keeper,
Admires your submissive beauty.

It is thanks to fortune and mankind
That you learned of secret joy,
Learned wordly ways: they call
All our joys betrayal. Betrayal becomes you.

The irrecoverable blush of shame
Has flown from your young cheeks.
Just so does Aurora's ray flee
Young roses, abducting their pure fragrance.

So be it! In scorching summer heat
Sense is tempted and eye enticed
To see blood flashing in shadows
Out from dense green in clustering grapes.

THE FINAL CATACLYSM 🔊

When the final hour of nature strikes,
The body of earth will be destroyed:
The waters again will mantle the land,
And God's image hover over them.

🔊

Bright day still clamored,
Streets sparkled with crowds,
And evening cloud-shadows
Flew past the shining roofs.

All teeming life's sounds
Reached me together—
All melted to one,
Clamorous, boistering, blended.[12]

Of spring pleasures weary,
I sank to sleep;

---

[12] Literally, "indistinct" or "confused."

How long I know not,
But strange indeed was my waking.

Stilled was the clamor,
And silence now reigned;
Shadows and flickerings
Were creeping along the walls.

The pale moon stealthily
Peered through my window,
And it seemed to me
It had been guarding my slumber.

And it seemed to me
That a peace-bringing spirit[13]
Had drawn me from brilliant
Gold day to the Kingdom of Shadows.

EVENING 𝄐

How quiet the distant bell's peal
Winding over the valley,
Like the murmur of flocking cranes
It fades in the rustling of leaves.

Like a vernal sea in flood,
The bright day does not waver,
Until hasting silent shadows
Spread wide across the valley.

MIDDAY 𝄐

Misty midday lazily breathes,
The river lazily rolls,
And in the pure flaming firmament
Clouds lazily melt away.

Warm somnolence, like a looming haze,
Embraces all of nature,
And now great Pan himself unruffled
Dreams in the cave of the nymphs.

[13] I have dropped Tyutchev's adjective "invisible," applied to the spirit, for rhythmic reasons.

THE SWAN 𝕤

Let the eagle flying beyond
The clouds greet lightning flashes
And with its staring eyes
Drink in the light of the sun.

No fate is more to be envied
Than yours, immaculate swan—
Divinity has dressed you
In features as pure as yourself.

Between the twin abysses
She nurses your allseeing dream;
You are everywhere surrounded
By the glory of starlit creation.

𝕤

You saw him in high society's world:
He was now whimsically gay, now glum,
Now carefree, now frowning, or with secret thoughts filled.
Such is the poet—whom you despised!

Regard the moon: like a wizened cloud,
It can scarcely last in the skies through the day.
Night comes, and then, a light-flashing god,
It shines upon the sleeping groves.

𝕤

In a mob of men, during day's coarse clamor,
My eyes, my gestures, reactions, and words
Dare not exult at meeting you.
My soul, do not therefore accuse me.

See how in daylight the light-flashing moon,
All misty-white, will dawn in the sky.
Night comes, and upon an immaculate glass
Sweet-scented amber oil will drip.[14]

𝕤

Just as ocean encircles the globe of earth,
Just so is our earthly life encircled by dreams;

---

[14] The reference is to holy oil and an icon-glass.

And then night comes, and with their sounding waves
The elements strike against its shores.

Its voice compels us and beseeches.
A magic skiff already stirs at the wharf,
The tidal water swells and quickly bears us
Into dark waves' immensity.

The celestial vault in starry glory
Cryptically watches us from out its depths,
While we drift ever onwards, a flaming abyss
On every side encircling us.

THE SEA STEED 𝕾

O zealous steed, O sea steed,
Cresting white and green,
Now mild and tender-tame,
Now furious and frisky!
By the seething whirlwind were you suckled,
In boundless heavenly fields;
It taught you how to spin,
To play, to leap at will!

I love you when you headlong rush
In all your prideful power,
Your thick mane all dishevelled,
Your body steaming and lathered,
And in a roaring run at the shore,
Gayly neighing, whirl,
Fling hooves on sounding strand,
And splinter into spray.

𝕾

Here where the indifferent vault of heaven
Regards an earth grown gaunt;
Here, plunged in a persistent dream,
Exhausted nature sleeps.

Only occasional white birches,
Stunted bushes, and moss

36

That has grown grey like agued visions
Disturb the deathlike stillness.[15]

CALM 🔊

The thunderstorm had passed. Still smoking
The lofty oak lay, by Peroun's bolts slain.
A grey-blue shadow rushed from its branches
All through the storm-refreshed vegetation.
Long since has the sonorous, engulfing
Song of the birds been sounding throughout
The grove, and the end of the rainbow's arch
Been anchored in the verdant crests.

TO TWO SISTERS 🔊

I saw you both together,
And I espied you entire in her—
The mildness of eyes, the softness of voice,
The charm of dawning day
That your presence always meant.

As though in a magic mirror,
It all appeared anew:
The sorrow and joy of days long past,
That youth of yours long gone,
That perished love of mine.[16]

MADNESS 🔊

There where the vault of heaven smokelike
Has blended with parched earth,
There, in joyful heedlessness,
A wretched madman lives.

Burned by incandescent rays,
Buried in flaming sands,
With glassy eyes he seeks for something
Above, among the clouds.

Then suddenly livened, with sensitive ear
Pressed to the heat-cracked earth,

[15] The poem was written at the time of Tyutchev's trip to Russia from Munich in May 1830.
[16] Who the "two sisters" were has not so far been ascertained.

He greedily attends, a cryptic
Contentment writ on his brow.

He thinks he hears a seething stream,
That he hears the current of underground
Waters and their lullaby songs,
And from earth a rumble rising.[17]

THE WANDERER

Zeus's sacred shelter protects
The poor wanderer who has pleased him.
Exiled from domestic hearths,
He is the blessed gods' guest.

This astounding world their hands have created
In its varied diversity
Lies open before him for his pleasure,
His profit, and edification.

Through villages, through towns, through fields,
The radiant road drifts on.
All earth is open to him. He sees
It all and glorifies God.

CICERO

The orator of Rome did speak
Amid alarms and civil wars:
"I rose late and on my way
Was overtaken by Rome's night."
That we know. But bidding farewell
To the glory of Rome, from the Capitoline
Hill you saw its bloody star.
Setting at last in all its grandeur.

Blesséd be the visitor
Of this world in its moments of destiny:
He is the one the gracious gods
Have bid to the company of their feast.

---

[17] The title of the poem is *Bezumie*, literally "madness" or "frenzy." The "madman" of l. 4 is *bezumye*, literally "madman," or "one in a frenzy." Tyutchev may have had the connections between art and nature in mind, taking *Bezumie* to refer to the poetic frenzy.

He has witnessed their exalted pageants,
He has been admitted to their council,
And drunk immortality from their cup,
A dweller in Heaven while still alive.[18]

I tracked across Livonian fields,[19]
All was so drear about me.
Colorless sky, sandstone earth—
All aimed at my pensive soul.

I remembered the sorrowful past of this land,
Its bloody, somber season,
When its sons, prostrate in the dust,
Licked foes' knightly spurs.[20]

And looking at you, wilderness river,[21]
And at you, waterside grove,
I thought: You came from far away,
As aged as this past.

So be it! By you alone could it[22] reach us
From the shores of another world.
O if only you would accord me the answer
To a single question about it!

But nature keeps silence about the past,
With a secret, ambiguous smile,
As a lad who has luckily witnessed night's charms
Keeps silence about them by day.

Knee-deep the shifting, sucking sand . . .
We ride; it is late; day fades;

[18] Pigarev suggests that "Cicero" was provoked by the July 1830 Revolution in France. However, the poem seems to me to be less political than ruminative.

[19] Written in October 1830 while Tyutchev was traveling back to Munich from Petersburg. Livonia, of course, is the medieval name for Latvia and Estonia.

[20] A reference to the time when Livonia was under the domination of the Teutonic knights of the Hanseatic League.

[21] The Dvina.

[22] The past.

The shadows of pines beside the path
Have already fused together.
Blacker and thicker the deep pine grove:
How melancholy these regions!
The louring night, like a hundred-eyed beast,
Stares out of every bush.[23]

AUTUMN EVENING 🖝

The serenity of autumn evenings
Retains a tender, secret charm:
The presaging luster of motley trees,
Purple leaves lightly, languidly rustling,
The hazy, quiet azure sky
Above lamenting orphaned earth,
And, like an augur of coming storms,
An occasional gusty, chilling wind,
A waning, a languor—and over all
That gentle, yearning, fading smile
That in rational creatures we call
Suffering's modesty divine.

LEAVES 🖝

Let pines and firs
Bristle all winter,
While muffled in snows
And blizzards they sleep.
Their spiny verdure,
Like hedgehog needles,
Will never yellow,
But never be fresh.

An ephemeral tribe,
We flower and sparkle,
And a little time
Are guests on dry boughs.
All the fine summer

[23] Also probably written on Tyutchev's return journey to Munich.

40

We were in beauty,
We played with sunbeams
And bathed in the dew.

But birds now are songless,
And bloomless the flowers,
Beams turned pale,
And zephyrs departed.
Why do we vainly
Droop and yellow?
Should we not rather
Fly after them?

Faster, still faster,
O wanton winds!
Still faster pluck us
From these tiresome branches.
Pluck us and whirl us,
We would not wait.
Fly, fly!
We will fly with you!

That day, I remember, for me
Was the dawn of life itself:
Silent she stood before me,
Her breast undulating,
Cheeks glowing, like a sunrise
Torridly blazing and burning.
And then a golden avowal
Of love, like the newborn sun,
Erupted from her breast—
And I beheld a new world![24]

MALARIA

I love this wrath divine, I love this secret
Evil invisibly flooding all things—flowers,

---

[24] Pigarev's note suggests that this poem was addressed to the same person as "Two Sisters."

Spring waters transparent as glass, rays iridescent,
And even the very sky of Rome itself.
A constant lofty, cloudless firmament,
Your breast constantly, sweetly, gently breathing,
This constant warm wind swaying the crests of trees,
This constant scent of roses—and all is Death!

We know there well may be in nature sounds,
Fragrant odors, flowers, and even voices
That harbinge the last of all our hours for us,
Bringing us pleasure in our final torments.
With them the fateful Minister of Judgment,
When he calls the sons of Earth out of this life,
Screens his features as with a diaphanous veil,
Aye! hides his terrible, awesome advent from them.

SPRING WATERS 🐦

The snow still lies white in the fields,
But the waters already murmur of spring;
They woo, they rouse the sleepy shores,
They woo and flash and speak aloud.

They speak aloud on every hand:
"Spring is coming, spring is coming!
We are the envoys of oncoming spring,
It has sent us in advance of it!"

Spring is coming, spring is coming!
And the redcheeked, lightfoot choral dancers
Of quiet, mild, Maytime days
Gayly press and throng behind it.

SILENTIUM 🐦

Be silent, be secret, hide
Your feelings and your dreams.
Deep in the depths of your soul
Let them mutely rise and set,
As clear stars do in the night:
Admire them and be silent.

How does a heart speak out?
How explain yourself to another?
Will he grasp what you live by?
Pronounced thought is a lie.
Your burrowing troubles the waters:
Drink of them and be silent.

Know how to live within—
Your soul contains a world
Of mysterious, magical thoughts;
The outer tumult stifles,
The beams of daylight blind:
Hear their song and be silent.

Just as scrolls smoke and flame
Above the incandescent coals,
And the hidden, muffled fire
Devours every word and line;

So my life sadly smoulders
And every day drifts off in smoke;
So bit by bit I die
In dullness unendurable.

O Heaven, if only once
This flame in freedom could uncoil,
And pining nor writhing no more,
I could flare up—and die!

SPRING CALM

O do not consign me
To sodden earth;
Hide me, inter me
Among dense grasses!

Let the breath of the breeze
Set the grasses stirring,
Pipes play afar,
And gentle bright clouds
Drift over me!

ON THE OCCASION OF GOETHE'S DEATH[25] 🔊
[Translator's title]

You were the best of all its leaves
On humanity's lofty tree,
Bred by its purest sap, matured
By the purest ray of the sun.

In constant consonance, your soul
Was one with its great soul.
Prophet-like, you spoke with storms
Or gaily with zephyrs played.

No late spring wind nor raging summer shower
Tore you from your natal branch:
Better were you and longer-lived than most,
And fell from the garland in your own time.

PROBLÈME[26] 🔊

The boulder rolled down the mountain lies in the valley.
How did it fall? No one now knows.
Did it break *itself* away from the heights
Or was it *hurled down by another's will*?
Age after age has scudded past,
And no one yet has answered the question.

A DREAM ON THE SEA 🔊

Sea and storm were tossing our boat;
Dreaming I drifted with every wave's whim.
Two infinities were in me,
And both capriciously inwardly played.
Around me the rocks were sounding like cymbals,
The winds were calling and the billows sang.
I lay deaf to this chaos of sounds,
But my dream rose over this chaos of sounds.
Painfully clear, magically mute,

[25] Goethe died in March 1832. Goethe was one of Tyutchev's favorite poets; he translated quite a number of Goethe's poems, including short pieces from *Faust*.
[26] The title in the original is in French.

Its light spread over the thundering dark.
In rays of fire it unfolded its world:
The earth grew green, the ether glistened,
Labyrinthine gardens, pillars, and halls,
And hosts of silent throngs were swarming.
I found many faces unknown to me,
I saw magical beasts, mysterious birds,
I strode like a god past celestial creations,
And the world shone motionless beneath me.
But through my dreams, like a sorcerer's howl,
I heard the crashing abyss of the sea,
And into my quiet vision's domain
Squalling billows' spume burst anew.

THE SKALDIAN HARP 𝄞

O Skaldian harp! Long have you slept
In the shadows of a dusty, forgotten corner;
But let the azure light of the moon,
Subduing the darkness, flash into your corner,
And a splendid sound soon throbs in your strings,
Like the raving of a soul affrighted in dreams.

What life did it evoke for you?
Did it remind you of days of yore,
Of how here once the melodies
Of sensuous maids at nighttime echoed,
And in these gardens still flowering
Their light feet glided with invisible step?

𝄞

I love the service of Lutherans,
Their rite so stern, so weighty, so simple.
I understand the sacred teaching
Of these naked walls, this empty temple.

Do you not see? Prepared for farewell,
This is the last time faith attends you:
She has not yet traversed the threshold,
But already her house stands empty and naked.

She has not yet traversed the threshold,
Not yet closed shut the door behind her.
But the hour is striking. Pray to God,
This is the last time for you to pray.

From land to land, from town to town,
Fate like a whirlwind hurls man along,
And joyous you be, or without joy,
What does she care? Forward, forward!

The wind brings us a familiar refrain:
It is the last farewell of love.
Behind us are many, many tears,
Before us fog and obscurity.

"O look about you, a moment stay,
Where would you flee, why would you flee?
The love you abandoned still remains,
Where in this world will you find one better?

The love you abandoned still remains,
In tears, despondency in its breast.
It is so wrung by all its sorrows,
Spare it a dram of felicity!

Recall unto your memory
The bliss of so many, many days.
All now that's dear unto your soul
You will abandon on your way!"

This is no time to rouse these shades:
Somber enough is the present hour.
The forms of the dead are more fearsome just
Because they were dear to us when they lived.

From land to land, from town to town
A mighty whirlwind hurls man along.
And joyous you be, or without joy,
What does she care? Forward, forward!

I remember a golden time,[27]
I remember a heartdear land.
Day was fading; we were two;
The Danube murmured in shadows below.

And on the hill, there where the ruin
Of a whitening castle gazes away,
You, a youthful fairy, stood,
Leaning against the mossy granite.

Your childlike foot was gently poised
Upon the pile of eternal debris;
The sun was dawdling, taking leave
Of hill, of castle, and of you.

A quiet transitory wind
Pursued its playing with your dress.
The falling blossoms of crabapple trees
Wove garlands about your youthful shoulders.

Your heart was light as you gazed afar.
Sun-rays had dimmed sky's marge in haze;[28]
The day burned low; the river louder
Was singing between its fading shores.

Carefree, joyous, and light of heart,
You waved farewell to that heavenly day;
And the shadow of swiftly flowing life
Floated sweetly over us.

Why are you wailing so, night wind?
Why do you keen and cry so wildly?
What does your strange voice signify,
Now silent in grief and now in grief roaring?

---

[27] Addressed to the Baroness Amalia Krudner, née von Lerchenfeld (1808–88). Tyutchev met her during his first year in Munich and evidently was infatuated with her. She married in 1825. Tyutchev wrote the poem some nine years later.

[28] Literally, "The edge of the sky was smokily extinguished in [the sun's] rays."

47

In a language the heart alone comprehends
You repeatedly speak of incomprehensible torment.
You rummage in the heart and, rummaging,
From time to time explode these frantic tones.

O do not sing these fearful songs
Of ancient chaos, of primal chaos!
How avidly the night-soul's world
Hearkens to its favorite tale!
It strives to escape its mortal breast,
It thirsts to merge itself with infinitude.
O do not rouse the storms that now are sleeping:
Chaos still is restlessly stirring beneath them.

The torrent has thickened and now grows dark,
Concealed beneath the solid ice,
Color fades and sound grows mute
In icy, numbing rigidity.
Almighty cold can paralyze all
Except th'immortal spring of life:
It flows on always and, babbling, gurgling,
Disturbs the deathlike silence.

So in a breast become a wasteland,[29]
Killed by the cold of earthly being,
Vivacious youth ceases to flow,
The sportive current ceases to shine.
But underneath the icy crust
There still is life, still murmuring,
And we may sometimes plainly hear
Mysterious whisperings of spring.

In the stifling stillness of air,
As though in foreboding of storm,
The roses' fragrance is sweeter,
And clearer the dragonfly's voice.

---

[29] Literally, "an orphaned breast."

48

Hark! Muffled thunder rolls
Behind the smokewhite clouds;
The sky is girdled round
By flying lightning flashes.

Life in overabundance
Infusing the sultry air,
Like the nectar of the gods
Thrills and burns in my veins.

Maiden, maiden, what causes
The swell of your young breasts?
What is it that dulls, what saddens
The moist luster of your eyes?

What is it that, paling, numbs
The flame of your maiden cheeks?
What is it that contracts
Your breast and scorches your lips?

Through your lowered silken lashes
Two tears have made their way.
Or are they the early raindrops
Of a storm about to begin?

Willow, why do you bend
Your crown above the waters?
And with your tremulous leaves,
Like so many thirsty lips,
Catch at the running stream?

Although your every leaf yearns
And trembles above the stream,
The stream still splashes and races,
And basking in the sun,
Glitters and laughs at you.

A misty, gloomy evening:
Could that be a skylark's voice?

Is it you, lovely guest of morning,
At this tardy, lifeless hour?
Supple, sportive, clear,
At this lifeless, tardy hour,
Like the awful laughter of madness
It jolted all my soul!

The casket is lowered into the grave
And all the crowd throngs round.
They elbow in, their breathing strained,
Breast squeezed by the scent of decay.

And over the still uncovered grave,
Above the casket's head,
A learned dignified pastor stands
Pronouncing obsequies.

He speaks of man's mortality,
His Fall, the blood of Christ;
Wise and proper is his speech,
Intriguing all the crowd.

The sky remains incorruptibly pure,
Endless above the earth,
And keening birds soar and float
In the airy blue abyss.

The east grew light, our boat was rolling,
The sail was joyously sounding.
The sea, like a sky turned upside down,
Was spinning under us.

The east grew red. She was praying,
Her veil from her forehead flinging,
Her lips were breathing her prayer, and heaven
Exulted in her eyes.

The east flared up. She inclined,
Her lustrous neck bowed low,

And all along her youthful cheeks
Fiery droplets streamed.

The world, at sunrise arisen,
Twitched like a little bird.
Alas! it is only I
Whom blessed sleep has passed by.
Though morning coolness blows
Through my disheveled hair,
Still I feel weighing upon me
Yesterday's heat and dust.

O how harsh and rude
How odious to me
Is the clamor, shuffling, shrieking
Of this newborn flaming day!
Its rays are red as blood,
Caustically burning my eyes.
Night, night, where is your shelter,
Your soothing shade and dew?

Remains of past generations
Who have survived your time,
How just is the unjust blaming
Of your complaints and groans!
How sad it is to struggle,
A drowsy, exhausted shade,
Onward to sun and progress
Behind a new generation!

My soul, Elysium of shades,
Shades silent, luminous, and lovely,
Out of touch with the thoughts of our raging time,
Out of touch with its joys, out of touch with its griefs—

My soul, Elysium of shades,
What tie is there between life and you?

Between you, phantoms of best days past,
And this insensible mob of our time?

❧

Golden clouds are drifting
Above the vine-covered hills.
The darkling river's green waves
Are murmuring below.
Gently eyes, from the valley
Rising, scale the heights
And see on the point of the peak
A circular temple shining.

There in that mountain dwelling,
No place for mortal life,
Currents of air, of mankind
Cleansed, more lightly meander.
Sound, flying there, grows mute,
And only nature's pulse
Is there, and something festive
Ranging, like Sunday stillness.

❧

There where the skipping mountains stretch
To shining plains
Th'eternal stream
Of celebrated Danube flows.

They say that there in olden times
On dark blue nights
A fairy chorus
Would shimmer in and through the waves.

The moon would listen, waves would sing,
And knightly castles
Perched on crags
Would gaze at them in delighted awe.

Isolated lights, imprisoned
In antique towers,

Winked back and forth
With unearthly, otherworldly rays.

The stars in the sky, one after another
In order gliding,
Would note them and slyly
Pursue their private colloquy.

All chained within his ancient armor,
The guard on the wall,
Mysteriously charmed,
Heard distant thunder as though dreaming.

But once he was lost in dreams thunder
Would clear and crash.
He would awaken
With prayers and then pursue his round.

No more. The years have taken all.
You have succumbed
To fate, O Danube:
Now steamboats sluggishly puff along you.

I sit pensive and alone,
I gaze through tears at a fireplace
    Long since darkened.
I find no words in my despair
To accommodate my anguished thoughts
    Of time long past.

Time long past—when was the past?
The present—will it be forever?
    It will pass.
It will pass as all has passed
And vanish in the somber chasm,
    Year after year.

Year after year, age after age . . .
Why should man, this earthborn reed,
    Be indignant?
He quickly, quickly withers, yes,

But with new summers there are new reeds
　　And other leaves.

All that is will be anew,
The rose's bloom will be anew,
　　And its thorns.
But you, my poor, my pallid bloom,
There will be no renewal for you,
　　No blossoming.

You were plucked by my own hand,
And with a joyful pleasure and anguish
　　God only knows!
Stay then close beside my heart,
So long as love's last sigh still lingers
　　On within it.

With reason is Winter vexed,
　　Her season has passed away.
Spring now knocks at the window
　　And gambols about the yard.

All has begun its playing,
　　All forces Winter away;
Even the larks in the sky
　　Have raised a peal of bells.

Winter still busily fusses
　　And growls and grumbles at Spring.
Spring heartily laughs in her face,
　　And Winter blusters still more.

The wicked witch was enfrenzied,
　　So quickly seizing some snow,
While running away she flung it
　　Against the beautiful babe.

Spring was but little grieved:
　　She washed herself in the snow
And only glowed the more,
　　Defying her enemy.

No, I have no power to hide
My passion for you, O mother earth.
True son of yours, I do not crave
The incorporeal lusts of spirits.
What are the joys of Paradise
Compared with you, with love, with spring,
The blossoming delights of May,
The glowing light, the golden dreams?

All day, in depths of lethargy lost,
To drink long draughts of warm spring air,
From time to time to follow the track
Of clouds in the pure and lofty sky;
To wander carefree, without aim,
And in a wood, by accident,
To chance upon the fresh aroma
Of lilacs or a vision clear.

How sweetly does the dark green garden drowse,
Languorously embraced by deep-blue night,
How sweetly does the golden moon shine through
The apple tree, with blossoms whitened.

As on creation's primal day, a host
Of stars mysteriously burns in a limitless sky,
We hear articulation of distant music,
And also the louder speaking of a nearby spring.

A veil has descended upon the diurnal world;
Motion has been stilled, toil fallen asleep.
Above the sleeping town, as in forest crests,
A strange nocturnal humming has been roused.

Whence does it come, this incomprehensible humming?
Is it the fleshless, heard but invisible world
Of mortal thoughts emancipated in sleep
That now is swarming in the chaos of night?

Grey shadows have blended together,
Color faded, sound fallen asleep.
Life, movement, both have dissolved
In shifting twilight, in distant droning.
Now may the sound of the moth be heard
Invisibly flying through the night air.
This is the time of ineffable anguish—
All in me, and I in all.

Quiet, sleepy twilight,
Invade the deepest depths of my soul,
Quiet, languid, scented,
Invade all things and calm them all.
Inundate my senses all
And bring the mists of oblivion.[30]
Let me taste annihilation,
Merge me with your somnolent world.

How wild the gorge!
Its stream is hasting towards me;
It hurries to the camp in the dell.
I climb upwards to where the fir tree stands.

The summit mounted,
I sit here, joyous, calm.
Now hurry, stream, to the men in the valley—
Try how great your strength may be with them!

A kite ascended from the glade
And rapidly sped into the sky;
Still higher, still further, on it soars,
And now is gone beyond the horizon.

[30] Literally, "self-forgetfulness."

Mother nature gave to it
Two mighty, two mercurial wings,
While I stand here, in sweat and dust,
I, lord of earth, stuck fast to earth!

THE FOUNTAIN 𓆸

How like unto a living cloud
The radiant, sparkling fountain writhes;
How its damp smoke first blazes up,
Then burns to powder in the sun.
It rises beam-like to the sky,
It touches the forbidden heights,
And then is fated to fall to earth
Anew in fiery-tinted ashes.

O cascade of mortal thought,
O inexhaustible cascade!
What law beyond our understanding
Impels your striving, then casts you down?
How avidly you dart to heaven!
But a fateful hand, hidden from sight,
Refracting your persistent beam,
Gleams in the spray from heights above.

𓆸

My soul would like to be a star,
Not when those lights like living eyes
Gaze down from out the midnight sky
Upon the sleeping world of earth,

But rather by day when, hidden as though
By smoke in the scorching rays of the sun,
Like deities they brighter burn
In the ether invisible and clear.

𓆸

Bright snow shone in the valley.
The snow has melted and gone.

57

Spring grass gleams in the valley.
The grass will fade and go.

But what age glows white there,
Upon the snowy heights?
Even now the sunrise
Sows fresh roses on them.

Nature is not what you suppose:[31]
Its soul is neither cruel nor blind.
It has a soul and liberty,
It has a tongue, in it is love.
. . . .
Behold the leaf and bud on the tree:
Was it a gardener who glued them there?
Do seeds mature in maternal wombs
By play of alien, foreign forces?
. . . .
They do not see and do not hear,
They live in darkness while in this world,
They never feel the breath of the sun,
Nor know of life in the waves of the sea.

Light has not entered into their souls,
Spring has not flowered in their breasts,
Woods have not spoken in their presence,
And the starry night is dumb to them.

The thunderstorm whose unearthly speech
Disturbs the rivers and shakes the woods
Has never taken counsel at night
With them in friendly conversation.

Not theirs the fault: let a deaf-mute catch
If he can the life of the organ tones.

---

[31] Stanzas two and four of this poem were forbidden by the censor when
the poem was printed in 1836, probably because of the implied pantheism of
the poem as a whole which these lost stanzas may well have made explicit.
There is no manuscript copy of the poem extant.

Alas! not even a mother's voice
Can rouse concern within his soul.

Still mournful is the mien of earth,
But the air already breathes of spring.
The dead stem quivers in the ground
And fir tree branches are stirring.
Nature has not yet awakened,
But through her slowly thinning sleep
She has discerned the coming spring
And cannot help her smiling.

My soul, my soul, you were asleep,
But what now suddenly excites you,
What caresses and kisses your sleep
And turns your dreams all golden?
Snow-blocks glitter and melt away,
The azure glitters, blood runs faster.
Is it the pleasure brought by spring,
Or is it perchance a woman's love?

There is no feeling in your eyes,[32]
There is no truth in your discoursing,
There is no soul in you.

Be brave, my heart, until the end:
There is no Creator in creation,
There is no point to prayer!

I love your eyes, my love,[33]
Their wonderful, passionate play
When suddenly you raise them

[32] Addressee unknown.
[33] Addressee unknown.

And boldly cast your glance,
Like skyborn lightning, about you.

But there is a mightier magic:
Of eyes to earth cast down
All through a fervent kiss,
And through the lowered lashes
The sullen faint flame of desire.

Yesterday in enchanted dreams,
The last ray of the moon
Upon your wearily winking eyelids,
You fell to tardy sleep.

Silence then surrounded you,
The shadow deeper frowned,
And the even breathing of your breast
Streamed louder through the air.

But not for long did gloom of night
Flow through the open window,
And flying to you, curl your locks,
And play with an unseen dream.

Now quietly flowing, quietly scudding,
As though by breezes borne,
Smokelight, mistylilywhite,
Something has flit through the window.

Now like an invisible being it darted
By the dimly shimmering rug,
Now grasping hold of the counterpane,
It clambered along the edges,

Now like a tiny serpent coiling,
It clambered upon the bed,
Now like a ribbon twisting, it straightened
Between the canopies.

In a sudden, palpitating blaze
It touched your youthful breasts,

And with a crimson stunning cry
Forced wide the silk of your lashes.[34]

JANUARY 29, 1837[35] 🐦

By whose hand did the deadly bullet
Pierce the poet's heart?
Who smashed this cup divine
As though it were an earthen vessel?
Whether he be innocent or guilty
In earthly justice's eyes,
The Most High's hand forever
Has branded him a *regicide*.

But you, who suddenly were swallowed
In timeless dark from light,
Peace to you, poet's shade,
Resplendent peace unto your ashes!
In all despite of men's vain words,
Your fate was great and holy:
You were the gods' living organ,
But burning blood was in your veins.

And with this noble blood you slaked
Your craving thirst for honor.[36]
You went to your repose
Shaded by banners of the people's grief.
Now let your foe be judged by Him
Who sees the blood you shed.
In Russia's heart you'll be
In mem'ry kept like a first love.

---

[34] In his book on Tyutchev (pp. 71–73), Richard A. Gregg insists upon
a Freudian interpretation of this poem.

[35] Pushkin was killed in a duel on January 29, 1837. Tyutchev's poem
was probably written later that year, possibly between May and July, at
which time he was in Petersburg.

[36] The duel was fought because of the attentions paid by Pushkin's oppo-
nent to Pushkin's wife.

DECEMBER 1, 1837[37] 🔊

Thus here it was that we were fated
To say our last farewell,
Farewell to all by which the heart lived,
Which first did kill your life, then burned it to ashes
Within your tortured breast.

Farewell. In many, many years
You, shivering, will remember
This land, this shore with its noontide radiance,
Perpetual brilliance and constant blooming,
Where the exhalation of late pale roses
Warms December's air.

ITALIAN VILLA[38] 🔊

Saying farewell to life's alarms,
Screened by a cypress grove,
In blissful shade, Elysian shade,
It[39] went to sleep betimes.

Two centuries or more ago,
Enclosed by a magical dream,
It retired to its flowering valley
And surrendered to Heaven's will.

But Heaven here is gracious to earth.
Summers and warm southern winters
Have often drowsily swept above it,
Their wings never rousing it.

The fountain still burbles in the corner,
A breeze strolls under the ceiling,
A swallow comes flying in and twitters,
It sleeps; its sleep is deep.

We entered: everything was calm,
For centuries peaceful and dim.
The fountain babbled. The motionless, graceful

---

[37] Probably occasioned by Tyutchev's separation, in Genoa, from Ernestine Dörnberg, a widow, who in 1839 was to become Tyutchev's second wife.
[38] Probably also connected with Dörnberg and Genoa.
[39] That is, the villa.

Cypress peered through the window.
. . . .
They all grew frightened: convulsive quivers
Ran through the cypress boughs.
The fountain fell silent. A certain strange murmur
Whispered[40] as though through sleep.

What is it, friend? Did the wicked life
That flowed in us then, that wicked,
Rebelling, passionate life, on purpose
Cross this holy threshold?

So long, so long, O blissful South,[41]
Since I saw you face to face,
Since you, like a god revealed,
Were accessible to me, a stranger.
So long since I—though not with rapture
Still not in vain with novel
Feelings filled—did listen
To the singing of great Mediterranean waves.

Their song, as *it has ever been,*
Was as perfect in harmony
As when from their natal womb
The shining Cyprian uprose.[42]
They have remained the same till now,
Glittering and sounding;
And over their azure plain
Holy apparitions glide.

But I, I bid farewell to you:
Anew am I northward carried.
Anew has its lead-colored sky
Been everywhere let down upon me.

[40] I have dropped the adverb "incoherently" here for rhythmic reasons.
[41] This is one of the first of Tyutchev's poems to make the contrast between the north and the south, to the advantage of the south.
[42] A reference to the legend of Venus' rising from the sea. Literally "the shining Cyprian floated."

Here air stings. There is heavy snow
On peaks and in the valleys.
Complete rule here is held
By almighty wizard cold alone.

But there, beyond this realm of snow-storms,
There, there at the marge of earth,
In the golden, shining South,
I still can see you far away:
Your glitter is lovelier by far,
Bluer and still more pure,
Your speech yet more concordant
Reaches unto my very soul.

With what sweet bliss and with what loving sorrow[43]
Your gaze, your ardent gaze, pined over him!
Insensately mute, as though you had been seared
  By heavenly lightning's fire.

Abruptly, with bursting heart, with feelings o'erflowing,
You trembled, dissolved in tears, and prostrate fell.
But soon good sleep, uncaring as a child,
  Lowered your silken lashes.

Your head inclined, you sank beneath its hand,
And it caressed you like a gentle mother.
A moan died on your lips. Your breathing smoothed.
  Your sleep was calm and sweet.

But this is now. O if you then had dreamt
Of what the future held in store for us!
You would have wakened wailing, as though wounded,
  Or passed to other sleep.

See how the west was flaming[44]
With glowing evening rays,

[43] The subject, again, is probably Tyutchev's parting from Dörnberg in 1837.
[44] This poem, written in 1838, could be read as political, contrasting Eastern and Western Europe.

While dimming east was dressed
In cold grey scales!
Are these two enemies?
Or is there a double sun
Which follows fixed decrees
And never will unite them?

SPRING 🍃

However heavy destiny's hand,
However deceit may torment man,
However wrinkles may furrow his brow,
However wounds may gash his heart,
Whatever may be the harsh ordeals
That you have had to undergo,
Still what can stand against these breezes,
Against a first encounter with spring?

Spring! Nothing she knows of you,
Nothing of you, nor evil, nor grief;
Immortal life gleams in her gaze.
There are no wrinkles on her brow,
Obedient to her own laws only,
She flies to you at appointed times,
Radiant, blissful, free of care,
As does become divinity.

Virginal as primal spring,
She scatters her flowers over the land;
She acknowledges no other springs
Which once there may have been before her:
Many a cloud is roaming aloft,
But all these clouds belong to her.
Never a single trace does she find
Of springs whose flowering life is over.

Not for the past do the roses sigh,
Nor nightingales at nighttime singing;

Not for the past does Aurora let flow
The fragrancy of her sweet tears.
Fear of the fated end awaiting
Rips none of its leaves away from the tree.
Their life, like an ocean knowing no shores,
Is all in the present moment expended.

Victim trapped by a personal life,
Come, renounce the deceits of the senses,
Courageously, with all your strength,
Plunge in this vivifying sea!
Come, in its light ethereal stream
Lave your tormented suffering breast,
Be part, if only for an instant,
Of that cosmic life we all may know.

DAY AND NIGHT 🖎

The lofty will of the gods has granted
That over the secret world of spirits,
Above th'anonymous abyss,
A gold-brocaded cloak be spread.
Day is this resplendent cloak,
Day, of earthborn the reviver,
The healer of deep-suffering souls,
The friend of men and deities.

But day is fading; night has come;
It has arrived; the fated world's
Bliss-giving sheltering cloak is rent
And cast away. Th'abyss is bared
To us in all its horror and gloom,
No barrier now is there between us—
And that is why night frightens us so.

🖎

Trust not, trust not the poet, maid;
He will not heed your call.
More than the flaming fire fear
The touch of a poet's love.

Never will you make his heart
One with your youthful soul;
You will not shroud his scorching fire
Beneath a wedding veil.

The poet, like th'elements, is almighty,
But powerless over himself;
He cannot keep his laurel crown
From searing youthful curls.

To no end does an inane people
Slander him or praise.
He does not snake-like sting the heart,
But sucks it like a bee.

The poet's pure hand will not infringe
Upon your sanctity,
But inadvertent will choke your life
Or bear you beyond the clouds.

Do not perplex the poet, I pray,[45]
With warm compassionate greetings
From the inaccessible heights of your place.
Do not seduce his dreams.

Lost all his life in the mob of men,
And sometimes exposed to their passions,
The poet, I know, is credulous,
But seldom serves powers that be.

His head is bowed whenever he passes
The idols of this earth,
Or else he stands confused before them,
Proud, but struck with dread.

But if of a sudden a living word,
Escaping their lips, should fall,
And through their earthly stateliness
A woman's charm should flash,

[45] Dedicated to the Grand Duchess Maria Nikolayevna, daughter of
Nicholas I, whom Tyutchev met at Tegernsee, near Munich, in 1840.

And if their beauty omnipotent
Is quickly, as by a blaze,
Illumined by human understanding,
Its features gracefully striking,

O how his heart does flame within him!
O how exalted, how touched!
Though he may not know how to serve,
He knows well how to worship.

❧

As I stood at the Neva I saw
The golden cupola
Of the Cathedral of Saint Isaac shining
Through the mist of a frosty fog.

Clouds were timidly ascending
Into the wintry night sky,
The frozen river was glowing white
In utter deathlike stillness.

Sorrowfully silent, I recalled
How in those lands the sun warms
Genoa's glorious, gorgeous gulf
Now blazes in the sun.

O North, O warlock-sorcerer North,
Have I been bewitched by you?
Or is my mind in truth enchained
By your granitic breadth?

O if a transient spirit, drifting
In quiet in evening mist,
Would only carry me quickly, quickly
There, there, to the warm South.

COLUMBUS ❧

To you, Columbus, to you the crown!
For you boldly completed the map of earth
And brought to final consummation

Th'unfinished business of the fates.
Divinely guided, you tore the veil
And out of the boundless misty expanses
To God's universe you brought with you
A new and unsuspected world.

Thus ever through the centuries
Has the reasoning power of man, united
Through common parentage, been bound
Together with nature's creative power.
Let him but speak the sacred word
And he will find that nature is always
Prepared to give response to the voice
Of its kindred kind with a new world.

🔊

I still aspire with yearning desire,[46]
I still surge toward you with my soul,
And in the dusk of memory
I capture still your form.
Your dear, your unforgettable form
Is everywhere and ever before me,
Beyond my grasp and always unchanging,
Like a star in the sky of night.

🔊

A shy reluctant sun
Looked down upon the field.
It thundered beyond the clouds,
The land began to darken.

Gusts of sultry wind,
Distant thunder and raindrops,
Cornfields turning green
And greener beneath the storm.

[46] Written in 1848, this poem was dedicated to the memory of Tyutchev's
first wife, who had died some ten years earlier.

A stream of livid lightning
Punched from behind the clouds;
A white and volatile flame
Formed a frame around it.

Faster fell the raindrops,
Dust whirling flew from the field,
And pealing rolls of thunder
Grew angrier and bolder.

Again the hov'ring sun
Cast eyes upon the field,
And th'agitated land
Was drowned in radiance.

So I encounter you again,[47]
Land though native no longer dear,
Where first my mind and feelings played,
Where now with dull and darkened eyes
The time of my childhood looks at me
In the light of a slowly fading day.

O poor phantom, now feeble, confused,
Of lost, enigmatic happiness!
Faithless, without pity now,
I look at you, my fleeting guest,
You are a stranger to my eyes,
Like an infant brother in his shroud.

Ah, no, not here, this desert land
Was never native to my soul;
Not here did bloom, not here was exalted
The festival of wonderful youth.
This earth does not contain the sum
Of what I lived by, what I treasured.

[47] Written in 1849, when Tyutchev, making a trip to Russia from abroad, paid a visit to his childhood home, Ovstug.

꙳

How stars glow red in the sky
On a quiet late summer night,
How drowsy cornfields ripen
In their crepuscular gleam.
How their golden, gilded waves,
Silently, sleepily dreaming,
By moon's rays whitened, sparkle
In the stillness of the night.

꙳

When in a circle of sickening sorrows
All turns us cold and life lies heavy
Upon us, like a stone, then suddenly,
God knows whence, our souls are consoled,
The past surrounds and embraces us,
And the frightful burden is momentarily lifted.

Just so sometimes, in the autumnal season,
When fields are empty and groves are bare,
The sky is pale and dales are dismal grown,
A sudden warm moist wind will blow,
Driving the fallen leaf before it,
And it is as though our souls were bathed in spring.

꙳

We followed our sure path
On the azure water's plain;
A firespitting, raucous
Seasnake bore us away.

Stars sparkled over us,
The wave was flashing below,
And it poured over us
A wet snowstorm of spray.

As we were sitting on deck
Many were vanquished by sleep.

The song of the wheels grew louder,
Raking the roaring billows.

Our merry circle grown quiet,
The womanish talk and tumult,
White elbows now support
Many dear and dreaming thoughts.

Dreams have scope to play
Beneath the magical moon,
And the peacefully flowing waves
Lull them with lullabies.

I see your eyes anew,[48]
And your southern gaze imbued
With sad Cimmerian night
Dispels this numbing cold.
Another land, a natal
Land, revives before me,
Like the Paradise the guilt
Of fathers destroyed for sons.

The waving rows of laurels
Ripple the skyblue air,
A gentle seaborn breeze
Relieves the summer heat,
The golden grapevine ripens
The whole of the day in the sun,
A fabled past wafts toward us
From under the marble arcades.

The fatal north has vanished
In a monstrous ugly dream,
And th'ethereal lovely vault
Of the sky shines over me.
With thirsty eyes I drink
Anew the bracing light

[48] The addressee of this poem is not known.

And under its pure rays
Discover a magic land.

🐾

Human tears, O human tears,
You flow at morn, and then at even,
You flow unknown, you flow unseen,
Limitless, beyond all counting,
You flow as streams of raindrops flow
In autumn, voiceless in the night.

🐾

O how he loved the fir trees[49]
That grow in his dear Savoy!
How musically their branches
Rustled over his head!
With what delightful thoughts
Their solemn louring gloom
And wild and doleful rustling
Charmed his understanding!

🐾

O how the column of smoke sparkles on high,
And how its elusive shadow glides below!
"That is our life," you calmly said to me,
"I mean not sparkling smoke so bright in the moon,
But rather this shadow seeking escape from smoke."

TO A RUSSIAN WOMAN 🐾

Far from nature and far from sun,
Far from light and far from art,
Far from life and far from love,

[49] The poem was written to Lamartine, who was born in Savoy. Tyutchev
had been much interested in Lamartine and in 1849, the year of composition
of "How he loved . . . ," wrote a four-line poem to Lamartine in French. As
early as 1822 he had translated Lamartine's "L'isolement" into Russian.

The years of your youth will quickly flash by,
Your vital senses all will perish,
Your dreams will all be blown away.

Unheeded will your life expire
In an unnamed and desert realm,
In a land no man has ever noted,
Vanishing like a cloud of smoke
In the hazy nebulous wastes of the sky,
In the limitless mists of autumn reaches.

Holy night ascended the horizon,
It wound consoling day around itself,
The gallant day, so like a golden cloak,
A cloak flung mantling over the abyss.
The world of sense departed like a vision.
Each man, so like a homeless orphaned child,
Now stands alone, feeble, frail, and naked,
Face to face with the somber bottomless pit.

Abandoned now entirely to himself,
His mind annulled, his reason meaningless,
And in his soul, as plunged in an abyss,
He finds no aid without, nor any bound.
And all once bright and vitally alive
Now seems to him to be a dream long past.
And in the alien unresponsive night
He recognizes his native legacy.

POETRY

Amid the thunders, amid the fires,
Amid the seething of our passions,
In elemental flaming discord,
From heaven she flies down to us,
Heaven-sent to the sons of earth,
An azure clarity in her gaze.
And over the mutinous rioting sea
She pours her reconciling oil.

ROME AT NIGHT 🦋

Rome reposes in the azure night,
All in possession of the risen moon
Which has imbued the sleeping city, stately
In loneliness, with her unspeaking glory.

How sweetly does Rome slumber in her rays!
How like to her are Rome's eternal ruins!
As though the lunar world and perished city
Were both one world—a magic world but dead!

VENICE 🦋

The Doge of a Venice free
Amid its azure swells,
Like a bridegroom in purple robes[50]
Was illustriously each year
In public rite espoused
With his Adriatic sea.

Not vainly did he hurl
His ring into these waters:
For ages, not mere years
(While all the nations marveled)
This leader's wonderworking
Seal bewitched and bound them.[51]

In love and peace the two
Acquired many glories.
Three centuries or four,
Its power ever growing,
The sail with its lion sign
Spread wide throughout the world.[52]

And now?
So many rings
Hurled to oblivious waves!

[50] Literally, "Like a regal bridegroom."
[51] The custom of this "marriage" of the Doge of Venice with the Adriatic continued until the end of the eighteenth century.
[52] Venice flourished from the twelfth through the sixteenth centuries.

75

Whole generations have passed:
And all these rings of betrothal,
These rings are no more now
Than links of weighty chains.[53]

The banquet was over, the singers silent,
The clay decanters had been emptied,
The baskets of fruit were overturned,
No dregs of wine remained in goblets,
And garlands now were crumpled on heads.
Now only stale aromas arise
In the bright, depopulated hall.
The banquet was over, we rose late.
Stars were shining in the sky,
The night had run through half its course,

While over the restless turbulent city,
Over the palaces, over the homes,
Over the street, its glowing lights
Opaque, its noisy moving traffic
And sleepless, insomniac[54] thronging crowds,
While over this terrestrial haze
The pure stars steadily were blazing
In the lofty limits beyond our reach,
Responding to our mortal sight
With their immaculate, spotless[55] rays.

Send, O Lord, your solace to him
Who in burning summer heat
Raves beggarlike beside the garden
Upon the parching pave;

[53] From 1814 to 1866 Venice was under Austria-Hungary. This poem
was written in 1850.
[54] I have added the redundant adjective for rhythmic reasons.
[55] I have added the redundant adjective for rhythmic reasons.

Who passing peeps over the wall at the shade
Of the trees, the grass of the vale,
At the coolness inaccessible
Of luxuriant shining meads.

Not for him do sheltering trees
Provide hospitable shade;
Not for him does the fountain hang
A misty cloud in air.

The azure grotto, as though from fog,
In vain invites his gaze.
And the fountain's dewy sprinkling spray
Does not refresh his head.

Send, O Lord, your solace to him,
Who wending his path through life,
Raves beggarlike beside the garden
Upon the parching pave.

ON THE NEVA

Yet once again a star submerges
In the rippling waves of Neva,
Yet once again does love entrust
Its secret skiff to her.

Between the ripple and the star
It glides as in a dream,
And bears two phantoms along with it
Far out along the wave.

Are they two children of festive ease
Here wasting an idle night?
Or are they rather two blissful shades
Forsaking the earthbound world?

O widely flowing as the sea,
Splendid streaming wave,
Grant refuge in your expanse to the secret
Borne by this simple skiff!

՜֎

However midday heat may waft[56]
In through the wide-thrown window,
Into this calm and tranquil temple
Where all is still and dim,

Where palpitating aromas wander
Among the dusky shadows,
Submerge yourself and now repose
In sweet halfsleeping dusk.

A nevertiring fountain here
Sings day and night in its corner
And sprinkles an enchanted mist
Of invisible droplets of dew.

And in the shimmering half light,
Seized by a secret passion,
Here softly wafts the gentle dream
Of a poet who is in love.

՜֎

Do not reason, do not plead:
Cretins judge and madmen seek.
The wounds of day are cured by sleep,
And tomorrow is as it will be.

While still you live, experience all:
Sorrow and joy and perturbation.
Desire what? And what regret?
Thank God, you have survived the day.[57]

՜֎

Beneath the foul weather's gusts
The swollen waters have darkened,

---

[56] Written in 1850, this is the first of Tyutchev's poems dedicated to Elena Alexandrovna Deniseva, who has often been called Tyutchev's "last love." According to Pigarev, this is the first of the so-called "Deniseva cycle" of love poems.

[57] The second quatrain plays four times on the word *zhit'*, to live: *zhivya*

78

Are covered with leaden veneer,
And through their dour gloss
A gloomy blood-red evening
Shines its sanguine ray.

It scatters golden sparkles,
It sows flamecolored roses,
And the torrent bears them away.
Above the dark azure wave
The flaming stormy evening
Tears its garland away.

Fanned by prophetic dreams,
The half-disrobed wood mourns;
But few of summer's leaves,
Now shining with autumn gilt,
Still rustle on the branches.

I watch with tender concern
When, breaching through the clouds,
A sudden lightning ray
Darts through the trees now mottled
With wan decaying leaves.

How delicate this aging!
What charm it holds for us
When what once bloomed and lived
And now is feeble and frail
Smiles for the final time.

TWO VOICES[58]

I

Courage, O friends, and struggle on,
Though biased the battle, the combat hopeless!

(living), *perezhit'* (experience), *tuzhit'* (sorrow), and *perezhit'* again (lives on).
  [58] This was one of Alexander Blok's favorite poems. Indeed, according to Pigarev, Blok had intended to use it for the epigraph to his play *The Rose and the Cross.*

The stars in the heights above you are silent,
Below you tombs—silent too.

Let gods on Mount Olympus disport:
Immortals know neither labor nor fear;
Only mortal hearts know labor and fear.
For them no triumph, but only an end.

2

Courage, struggle, O daring friends,
Though ruthless the battle and stubborn the combat!
Above you silent starry spheres,
Below you deaf and voiceless graves.

Let Olympians look with envious eye
At the combat waged by your stalwart hearts.
Fate conquers him who fighting falls,
But he wrenches the conqueror's crown from their hands.

See on the river's wide expanse,
On the reborn waters' flanks,
Icy floe drifts after floe
To the all-embracing sea.

Whether rainbow-flashing in the sun
Or in the late dark night,
They all, inevitably thawing,
Drift to a single goal.

They all together—small and large,
Of pristine form bereaved—
They all, dumb as the elements,
Dissolve in the fatal abyss.

O how our thought is tempted to ask:
You, the human I,
Is not your meaning such as this,
Will not this be your fate?

O how murderously we love,
How in passion's raging blindness
We kill the finest thing of all,
The dearest to our hearts!

How long since, preening in victory,
You said, "Ah, she is mine."
Not even a year. Now ask and learn:
What has survived of her?

Whence fled the roses of her cheeks,
Lips' smile and flash of eye?
The scalding moisture of her tears
Has seared, has burned it all.

Do you remember, at your meeting,
Your first, your fateful meeting,
The magic of her glance and speech,
Her maidenly lively laughter?

And what of now? Where is it all?
How lasting was the dream?
Alas! like summer in the north,
It was a transient guest.

Your love for her was a sentence dire
Imposed by destiny;
It set a seal of undeservéd
Shame upon her life.

Life abnegated, agonized life!
In the deepest depths of her spirit
Memories still remained to her.
But they betrayed her too.

The earth became a savage place
To her, enchantment fled.
The mob invading trampled in filth
The blossoms of her soul.

And what was left to her to treasure
Like ashes from her torment?

81

Pain, the evil pain of hell,
Unsolaced, tearless pain!

O how murderously we love!
How in passion's raging blindness
We kill the finest thing of all,
The dearest to our hearts!

𝓈❧

I do not know if grace will touch
My soul, by sin diseased,
If it will rise again restored,
If the swoon of my spirit will pass.

But if it happens that my soul
Does find its ease on earth,
Then you will have been grace to me,
My earthly Providence!

FIRST LEAVES 𝓈❧

The youthful leaf is greening,
See how the birches swaying
With youthful leaves stand tall,
Their gossamer green translucent,
Pellucid, transparent, like smoke.

Long were they dreaming of spring,
Of spring and golden summer,
And now these vivid dreams
Burst sudden into light
Beneath the first blue sky.

O beauty of first leaves,
Bathed in the rays of the sun,
With their shadows newly born!
Their movement lets us know
That in this myriad darkness
Not one dead leaf exists.

Oft have you heard me vow:[59]
"I am not worth your love."
Though she be my creation,
Still I am poor before her.

Thoughts of myself are pain
To me before your love.
I stand, am silent, I hallow
And make obeisance to you.

When at times tenderly
With passing faith and prayer,
You needs must bend your knee
Before the darling cradle

Where *she*, your nameless cherub,
Child born of you, is sleeping,
Accept then my submission
Before your loving heart.

OUR CENTURY

Not flesh but spirit has our time
Corrupted, and man despairing grieves.
He strives to light from the night shadows,
And finding light, complains, rebels.

By belief both burned and withered,
The unbearable he daily bears.
He recognizes that he is doomed,
He thirsts for faith, but will not *ask* it.

He will not say, in prayer and tears,
Before the bolted door amourning,
"Admit me, Lord! I believe, my God!
Come to the aid of my unbelief!"[60]

---

[59] Addressed to Deniseva soon after the birth of her eldest daughter, Tyutchev's child, in 1851.
[60] A paraphrase of Mark 9:24.

WAVE AND THOUGHT ꜱ

Thought after thought, wave after wave—
Two shapes of a single element.
Whether in the heart enclosed or in a limitless sea,
Whether it be here in prison or there in broad expanses,
Always this endless ebb and flow,
Always this troubled hollow ghost.

ꜱ

Still drenched with heat
The July night glittered,
Above dim earth
A storm-pregnant sky
Was quaking with lightning,[61]

As though heavy lashes
Were raised above earth,
And through lightning streaks
Someone's menacing pupils
Caught fire at times.

ꜱ

There is high meaning in our parting:
However you love—a day or an age—
Love is a dream, a dream is an instant,
And whether his waking be early or late,
A man must finally awake.

ꜱ

How gay the rumble of summer storms
When, flinging up the flying dust,
They threatening scud the clouds before them,
Disturb the azure of the sky,
And rashly, madly, of a sudden
Attack the grove of leafy trees.

[61] Literally, "with summer lightning."

Then all the grove begins to tremble,
Rustling through its broadleaved length.

How giants of the woodland bend
Beneath this heel invisible;
Uneasily their crests complain
As though consulting among themselves;
And through the sudden anxiety
The loudly calling birds are heard,
And somewhere the first of the leaves to yellow,
Spinning, flies onto the road.

Day fades to dusk, night nears,
The mountain's shadow lies longer,
Clouds die away in the sky.
It is late. Day fades to dusk.

I do not fear night's gloom,
Nor regret declining day,
If you, my magic phantom,
If you do not forsake me.

Shield me with your wing,
Soothe my heart's unrest,
Your shadow will be a blessing
For my enchanted soul.

Who? Whence? And how decide
Whether you are of heaven or earth?
Perhaps an ethereal being,
With a woman's passionate soul.

PREDESTINATION

Love, love, the legend runs,
Is soul united with kindred soul,
Their blending together, their conjoining,
Their fusion ever fated,
And fateful duel.

The tenderer one of them is
In the biased battle of these two hearts,
The more certainly and surely will it,
Loving, suffering, grieving,
Waste away.

Do not say he loves me as before,
That he does prize me as he did before.
O no! he barbarously destroys my life,
Although the knife is trembling in his hand.

Now wrathful, now in tears, pining, indignant,
Impassioned, stung unto my very soul,
I suffer, not live. In him, in him alone
I live, but this life—O how bitter it is!

He measures my air out carefully and meanly,
Not so is it measured for the fiercest foe.
Alas! I draw my breath in pain and toil,
I still can breathe, but can no longer live.

O do not trouble me with just reproach,
Your lot is far more envious than mine.
You love without disguise and ardently,
And I, I gaze at you with jealous spite.

A wretched wizard, I unbelieving stand
Before the magic world that I created,
And blushing I confess myself to be
The lifeless idol of your living soul.

What once with love you offered prayers to,
What once you guarded as though holy,
Fate changed into the blasphemies
Of human scandal-spreading talk.

The mob invaded, the mob broke in
Upon the temple of your soul,
You could not help but feel ashamed
At the secrets and sacrifices it gained.

O if only then the agile wings
Of the soul had soared above the mob,
They would have saved it from violation
By the people's undying banality.

I have known eyes—O those eyes!
And God knows how I loved them!
I could not tear my soul away
From their magic, passionate night.

In this gaze that passes understanding,
Baring her life to its depths,
I could perceive such grieving sorrow,
Such welling depths of passion!

Lamenting, grave, it deeply breathed
In her thick lashes' shadows,[62]
As though of pleasures weary, as though
These sufferings were fatal.

Not once did I encounter it,
In these miraculous moments,
Without a quiver of agitation,
Nor admire it without tears.

TWINS

Twins there are, two deities
For those of earth born—Death and Sleep,
As wonders of likeness as brother and sister.
She is more gloomy, milder he.

But other twins there also are,
No pair in the world is lovelier,

[62] Literally, "In the dense shadow of her lashes."

And no bewitchment is more awful
Than betrayal of the heart to them.

Their union is of blood, not chance,
And never but at fatal times
Do they enchant and fascinate us
With their insoluble mystery.

Who in profusion of sensations,
When blood in turn both seethes and freezes,
Has not been prey to your allurements,
You twins of Suicide and Love!

Mobile comme l'onde[63] 🙚

You, seawave of mine,
Wayward, willful wave,
Whether resting or at play,
How wonderfully alive—

Whether you laugh in the sun,
Reflecting the vault of the sky,
Or you tumble, thrash, and churn
In the waters' wild abyss.

Sweet your quiet rustling,
Replete with caresses and love;
I hear too your violent plaining
And your prophetic groans.

In the violent elements
Be you now gloomy, now clear,
But in your azure night
Preserve whate'er you've seized.

No ring as sacred gift
Did I hurl in your swell,
Nor was it precious stones
That I interred within you.

---

[63] Fickle as the wave. The manuscript copy of this poem has no epigraph. However, it was printed with the epigraph as a title in the collections of 1854 and 1868. Pigarev prints it as I have given it, without explanation.

No, at a fateful moment,
Drawn by your mystery,
My soul, my living soul,
I buried in the depths of you.

IN MEMORY OF V. A. ZHUKOVSKY[64] 🙚

1

I saw your evening. It was so beautiful!
As I took leave of you a final time,
I feasted my eyes upon it: quiet, clear,
And through it all a radiating warmth.
O poet, how they warmed and how they shone,
Your final radiant valediction rays.
Already had the first stars in his night
With striking clarity meanwhile appeared.

2

In him was no duplicity nor lying;
He rather reconciled and joined all things.
How kind and gracious was his friendliness
When he read Homer's tales aloud to me.[65]
The years when he was young and first beginning
Were years of blossoming and joyful hope.
Meanwhile the stars had vaulted over them
Their enigmatic, secret, dusky light.

3

In truth, his spirit, like a dove, was pure,
Unscathed; although he did not hold in scorn
The serpent's wisdom, and could understand it,
A purely dovelike spirit still blew in him.
And it was in this purity of spirit
That he grew up, was strengthened, and educated.
His soul was inspired unto harmony;
In harmony he lived, in harmony sang.

[64] Zhukovsky died on April 11, 1852, in Baden-Baden. Tyutchev wrote this eulogy the following July. Tyutchev had known Zhukovsky as a child and always retained his admiration for him.

[65] Zhukovsky's translation of the *Odyssey* was one of the most highly

4

It was this lofty harmony of soul
That formed his life and permeated his lyre
As finest fruit, and as his finest deed
That he bequeathed unto the restless world.
But will the world ensnare it, will it prize him?
Are we deserving of his holy pledge,
Or has divinity not said of us,
"None but the pure in heart shall behold God!"[66]

The sun is shining, the waters glitter,
A smile on all and life in all.
The trees are trembling in gladness and joy,
As they bathe their crests in the bluehued sky.

The trees are singing, the waters glitter,
The air is liquified in love.
The world, the flowering world of nature,
Is ecstasied by life's abundance.

But in this abundance of ecstasy
No ecstasy is any greater
Than just a single tender smile
Of your tormented, weary soul.

Enchanted by wizard winter
The sylvan forest stands.
Motionless and mute
Beneath its fringes of snow,
It sparkles with wonderful life.
And so it stands, enchanted,
Not dead, yet not alive,
By a magic dream bewitched.

----

regarded of his works.
[66] Matthew 5:8.

All is wound round, all fettered
By light and downy chains.

The winter sun will sweep
Its scything ray above it;
In it will be no trembling,
And all of it will flash
And sparkle in blinding beauty.

LAST LOVE 🙟

How much more superstitiously
And fondly[67] we love in declining years.
Shine on, shine on, O farewell blaze
Of my last love, of afterglow.

The shadows have spread across the sky
And only westward does radiance wander.
Linger, linger, evening–day,
Lengthen, lengthen, O enchantment.

Let blood run thin in veins, our fondness[68]
Does not run thin within our hearts.
O you, O you, O my last love!
You are my bliss and my despair.

SUMMER 1854 🙟

This summer, what a summer this is!
This is plain sorcery.
And was this given to us, I ask,
By no one, without source?

With anxious worried eyes I scan
This lustrous radiance.
Is it not making game of us?
Whence does this greeting come?

---

[67] That is, both tenderly and foolishly.
[68] "Tenderness" would be the better word here, but I have used "fondness" for rhythmic reasons.

Alas! just so the youthful smile
Of women's lips and eyes
Does not enrapture or allure us,
But confounds us in our age.

꙰

Alas! what is more powerless
And sadder than our ignorance?
Who dares to utter *until we meet*
Beyond a two or three day chasm?

꙰

The flame glows red, the flame flares up,
Sparks spatter and fly. But the garden
In darkness beyond the stream
Breathes coolness over them.
A twilight here, there heat and wailing,
I dreamlike wander, I feel
That only I am live:
You are with me and all in me.

Crash after crash, plume after plume,
The naked chimneys jut.
But calm, inviolate,
The foliage rustles and waves.
I, by their gentle breathing fanned,
Detect your passionate voice.
Thank God, I am with you,
And being with you is like Paradise.

꙰

Certain moments in life
    Are hard to portray:
They are the graceful moments
    Of the world's self-forgetting.
The forest's treetops murmur

High over me,
And only skyborne birds
Converse with me.
All things banal and false
Are gone afar.
All dear beyond my reach
Is close and gentle.
Pleasant and sweet to me
Is the world in my breast,
Drowsiness engulfs me—
Wait, O time!

༄

O you, prophetic soul of mine,
O heart o'erflowing with anxiety,
O how you struggle on the threshold
Of what does seem a double life!

You are a dweller in two worlds:
Your day is painful and passionate,
And prophetically vague are your dreams,
Like revelations of spirits and ghosts.

Let fatal passions rage and riot
In my afflicted, suffering breast:
My soul is ready, like Mary,[69] to cling
Forever to the feet of Christ.

༄

All I have managed to preserve,
Hope, faith, and love,
All fuse into a single prayer:
Live on, live on![70]

[69] Mary Magdalen.
[70] Written in 1856 to Tyutchev's second wife on her birthday.

TO N. F. SHCHERBINA[71] ❧

I fully comprehend
Your painful dreams,
Your struggle and your striving,
The trembling homage you render
To beauty's ideal.

Just so the Hellenic captive
At times asleep
On the steppe in Scythian snow,
In golden freedom wandered
In his Grecian sky.

❧

Above this ignorant mob[72]
Of an unawakened people,
When will you rise, O Freedom,
When will your golden ray shine?

Your ray will shine and rouse,
And scatter dreams and shadows.
But the ancient, putrid sores,
The scars of force and wrong,

The corruption of souls and the void
That gnaws at the mind and aches
In the heart, who will heal, who cover?
You, pure chasuble[73] of Christ.

❧

The season of early autumn
Is a short but wonderful time;

---

[71] Shcherbina (1821–69) was a minor poet whose poetry is full of ancient images and themes.

[72] This poem was occasioned by the Feast of the Dormition of the Virgin (Assumption of the Virgin in Roman Catholicism) in 1857, when Tyutchev was in Ovstug.

[73] The word for chasuble is *riza*, which can also mean the metal covering on an icon.

The day seems crystalline,
And the evening radiant.

Where brisk scythes played and cornspikes
Tumbled, now all is bare,
And only a spiderweb thread[74]
Now sparkles in the idle furrow.

The air is vacant, no birds
Are heard, the first winter storms
Are distant, and pure warm azure
Flows over the fallow field.

See how the grove is greening,
Glazed by the scorching sun,
And with what languorousness
Each branch and leaf is waving.

Let us go and sit above tree-roots
Watered by deep springs,
There, where, bathed in mists,
Spring whispers in speechless twilight.

Their crests rave over us,
Immersed in the midday heat,
And only a rare eagle cry
Reaches down to us from the heights.

Those hours when burdens
Lie heavy on breasts,
When hearts are weary
And darkness threatens,

When, still[75] and weak,
We are so grieved

---

[74] Literally, "hair."
[75] Literally, "motionless."

That even consolings
Of friends comfort not,

Then secret caresses
Of sunbeams find us
And, a glowing stream,
Pour on the wall;

From a kind shore,
From azure heights
Aromatic air
Blows through the window.

These bear no lessons
Nor counsels to us.
They do not save us
From fortune's slanders.

But we feel their strength,
Perceive their grace;
We grieve the less,
And easier breathe.

So much more kind,
So much more gracious,
Airy and clear,
Was your love to my soul.

She was sitting on the floor
Sorting a pile of letters;
She took them in her hands,
Then dropped them like ashes grown cold.

She took the familiar pages
And looked at them in wonder,
As souls look from their heights
At bodies they have forsaken.

O how much life was there,
Irrevocably lived!
O how many moments of sorrow,
Of love, of joy—all killed!

I stood in silence aside,
Prepared to sink to my knees,
And I grew dreadfully sad,
As though a dear ghost were watching.

PEACE 🖎

When all the things we called our own
Are gone from us forever,
And have become as heavy to us
As graveyard monuments,

Then let us go and cast our eyes
There, at the waterside,
There where the streams impetuous rush,
There where the torrent speeds.

In emulation of one another
They rush, the currents run
In answer to a fateful call
That they have heard far off.

In vain it is we follow them;
They will not come again.
But the longer that we go on gazing,
The easier we breathe.

And now the tears gush from our eyes
And through the tears we see
How all, in billowing and rolling,
Is quickly borne away.

The soul falls into heavy sleep,
And has the clear sensation
That an o'erpowering river wave
Is bearing it away.

🖎

I love the garden of Tsarskoe Selo[76]
In late autumnal days,

[76] Tsarskoe Selo was the summer residence of the tsars where Alexander I

When it is seized by silent mist,
As though by somnolence,
And whitewinged phantom swans
On the leaden mirror of the lake,
As though in pleasure swooning,
Rest torpid in this hazy mist.

And on the royal marble steps
Of Catherine's palaces
The twilight shadows of early October
At nightfall fall; the orchard,
Like a wooded glen, grows dark;
Beneath the stars, out of the night,
Like a gleam of ancient glory,
A golden cupola appears.

ON THE WAY BACK[77] 🐦

I

A grievous sight, a grievous hour;
The long way stretching drives us on.
See there: the moon has risen,
Sepulchral ghost, and illumined
A deserted mist-covered land.
    The way is long; do not lose heart.

O at this very selfsame hour,
There, where we no longer are,
That very moon, but live,
Breathes in Lake Léman's glass.
A wondrous sight and land.[78]
    The way is far; do not look back.

2

My natal scene: the distance blues
    Beneath a vast grey awning

---

had founded a lycée, which Pushkin attended. The first railway in Russia, constructed in 1838, was between Tsarskoe Selo and St. Petersburg.

[77] Written in 1859, the poem concerns Tyutchev's feelings on his way from Königsberg (now Kaliningrad) to Petersburg.

[78] Literally, "A wondrous sight, a wondrous land."

Of snowfilled clouds; a gloomy wood,
    Enwrapped by autumn haze.
All is so bare, deserted stretching[79]
    In mute monotony.
But patches of stagnant water glitter
    Beneath the early ice.

No sounds, nor color, nor movement here:
    All life is gone. To fate
Submitting, sunk in exhaustion's slumber,
    Man here dreams only himself.
Like this day's light, his eyes are dim,
    He cannot believe, though lately
He saw them, in lands where opaline mountains
    Look down on azure lakes.

DECEMBER MORNING

A moon in the sky: the shade
Of night is still unbroken;
She holds her reign unconscious
That day has already begun,

That shyly, lazily,
Ray after ray arises,
Though all the sky still burns
In celebration of night.

These moments soon will pass,
The night on earth will vanish,
And day's world will embrace us
In all its brilliant show.

TO E. N. ANNENKOVA

The life we lead from day to day
Holds joyful rainbow dreams;
To an unknown land, to a magic world,
Though strange to us still intimate,
They suddenly sweep us away.

---

[79] Literally, "so emptily immense."

99

Behold: from out the deep blue vault
It brings a different world[80]
To us, we see another nature,
And without rising, without setting,
Another sun shines there.

All there is truer, brighter, freer,
So far from earthly things,
So different from what is in our world;
And in the pure and flaming ether
So gently close to our soul.

We were awakened, the vision ended,
We had no means to keep it;
And with its wan and chilling shade,
Consigning us to prison anew,
Life once more embraced us.

But endlessly the subtle tone
Intones in skies above us,
And still the yearning, weary soul
Recalls that irresistible gaze,
That smile that is in dreams.

Although my home is in the valley,
Still there are times I feel
How bracingly the airy stream
Whirls wide upon the heights,
How breasts strive bursting to break out through
This strangling cover and thirst
For heaven's heights, how they would spurn
The smotherings of earth.

I gaze at the unattainable ridges
For hours at a time:
What cooling dews and singing breezes
Soar down to us from there!
Upon a sudden their spotless snows

[80] Literally, "a world not of this place."

With fiery color brighten;
The subtle steps of heavenly angels
Are passing by along them.

ON THE JUBILEE OF
PRINCE PETER ANDREYEVICH VYAZEMSKY[81] 🔊

The Muse's choices often change,
Her gifts are granted in varied measure;
More blissful than happiness is she,
But just as whimsical as it.

She fondles some but at their dawning,
She kisses their youthful silken curls,
But let a warmer breeze arise
And she will flee with their first dream.

At times in brooks and secret meadows
She unexpectedly appears,
Her random smile may give much joy,
But this first meeting will be all.

Not so were you condemned by her:
She seized upon you in your youth,
Fell deeply in love with your soul,
And long looked closely into you.

Not just in passing, but over time
She guarded, caressed, and cared for you,
She nursed your talent, and every year
Her love for you became more tender.

Just as the noble fruit of the vine
Grows stronger, flushing, with the years,
So brighter, warmer into your cup
Did inspiration ever flow.

And never with such wine as now
Was your renowned cup filled to crowning.

---

[81] This poem, written early in 1861, was read by P. A. Pletnyov at a banquet honoring Vyazemsky for fifty years of literary activity. Tyutchev and Vyazemsky had been close friends for many years.

So let us raise a brimming glass,
O Prince, in honor of this goddess,

The goddess' honor who nobly keeps
The pledge of all your soul holds holy,
Your native tongue. May she increase
And consummate her greatest deed.

Then all of us, in prayerful silence,
Will make an *in memoriam*,
A triple libation will we make
To three loves we will not forget.

There is no answer to the voice
That calls them, but on your namesday feast
We call those rare ones who are gone—
Zhukovsky, Pushkin, Karamzin!

We know that now, like unseen guests,
Their Mount Parnassus world forsaken,
They wander sympathetically
Among us, they sanctify this feast.

In name of your Muse, after them,
O Prince, we offer up this wine
To you. And may it many years
In this bright beaker bubble and flash!

O then it was I knew her,[82]
In legendary years,
When she was like a star
Which, faced with first light's rays,
Retreats in the azure sky.

And she was always full
Of that spontaneous charm,
That darkness just at dawn
When dew lies on the flowers,
Invisible and still.

[82] Whom Tyutchev had in mind is not known.

O all her life was then
Perfected so, so whole,
So alien to earthly being,
That she did flee, it seemed,
And hid like a star in the sky.

Play on, while over you[83]
The azure still is cloudless;
Play on with men, play on with fate,
For you are life, appointed to battle,
A heart athirst for storm.

How often, by sorrowful dreams
Fatigued, I gaze at you,
And then my eyes are dimmed by tears.
Why? What in common is there between us?
You go to life; I leave.

I never found my dreams
But at the break of dawn.
But later volatile thunderstorms,
But passion's bursts, but passion's tears—
No, these are not for me.

Perhaps in summer's heat
You will recall your spring.
O then remember of this time
How pensively until the dawn
We vaguely mused our dream.

ON SENDING THE NEW TESTAMENT[84]

No easy lot nor comforting
Was planned for you by fate,

---

[83] The addressee is not known.

[84] Written in 1861, to Tyutchev's elder daughter, Anna, who was at this time thirty-two years of age. The first stanza refers to the death of Anna's mother at her birth.

103

In childhood you entered unequal battle
With unrelenting life.

You fought with the fortitude of few,
And in this fateful battle,
Out of its most severe ordeals,
You brought your spirit whole.

No, life has not defeated you,
For in the deadly struggle
Not once, my friend, did you betray
The heart's truth or yourself.

But poor are all our earthly powers:
Life's ills rage ever greater,
And we, as on the brink of the grave,
Suddenly feel a dreadful weight.

Now when this happens, at these times,
Recall this book with love;
Press close to it with all your soul,
As to your pillow, and rest.

Some have received from nature[85]
Instincts prophetic and blind;[86]
They feel by them, hear waters
Below, in earth's dark depths.

Great Mother's beloved, your lot
Is most to be envied of all;
For oft have you beheld her
Beneath her outward veil.

TO N. I. KROL'[87]

The cold September was blustering
And rusty leaves were tumbling from trees,

[85] Written to the poet Afanasy A. Fet, probably in 1862. Fet, one of Russia's finest lyric poets, was a great admirer of Tyutchev's work.
[86] Literally, "prophetically blind."
[87] Krol' was a minor poet and dramatist of the time.

Haze drifted as daylight reached its end,
The night descended, mist arose.

Then for my eyes and for my heart
All was so colorless and cold,
All was so mournful and resigned,
When suddenly I heard a singing.

And then, as though a spell were cast,
The mist rolled up, then flew away,
The vault of heaven turned to blue
And was covered with radiance again.

All things were turned to green anew,
All things were changed into the spring.
This is the dream that then I dreamt,
All while your songbird was singing to me.

The *bise*[88] has died. More gently breathes
The azure host of Léman's waters.
The boat coasts over them anew,
The swan anew does ripple them.

All day the sun warms, as in summer,
The trees are spangled with motley colors,
The air in an affectionate wave
Caresses their decaying splendor.

And there, in solemn, grave repose,
Disclosed at morning to our view,
The distant peaks of Mont Blanc shine
Like an otherworldly revelation.

O here the heart might all forget,
Might here forget all, all its torment,
That it was there, in its native land,
That one grave made it ever less.[89]

[88] The north wind which blows across Lake Léman in the winter.
[89] The poem was written in Geneva in 1865. The last line refers to the grave of Deniseva in Petersburg. She had died on August 4, 1864.

A living magic breathes in her,[90]
Like a secret still unsolved.
In fearful trembling do we look
At her eyes' quiet gleaming.

Is it an earthly charm in her,
Or an unearthly grace?
The soul is fain to pray to her,
The heart bursts to adore.

O this South! O this Nice![91]
O how their brilliancy alarms me!
Life, like a bird a shot has wounded,
Would raise itself aloft, and cannot.
It cannot fly, nor can it range;
Its broken wings hang drooping down,
And pressing itself into the dust,
It quivers in pain and impotence.

She lay unconscious all day long[92]
With shadows mantling her;
A warm summer rain was streaming, its drops
Resounding gaily on leaves.

Awareness slowly came to her,
Her ear cocked to the din,
Long did she listen, captivated,
Submerged intent in thought.

[90] Dedicated to the Empress Maria Alexandrovna, wife of Alexander II.
[91] Written in Nice in 1864. Tyutchev lived in Nice from October 1864 to March 1865. Deniseva had died shortly before his arrival. Incidentally, Nice at the time was Italian, not French. Tyutchev could not bear France, despite his fondness for its literature and his fluency in its language.
[92] Written about the same time as "O this South . . . " and in reference to Deniseva's death.

As though conversing with herself,
All full aware she said
(I was by her, alive but killed),
"O how I loved all this!"
. . . .
You loved. To love as you did love—
No, no one has done that!
O Lord, how can this be survived
Without a broken heart!

How beautiful you are, night sea,
Here radiant, there grey and dark!
It moves beneath the gleaming moon
As though alive, and breathes, and shines.

Above its endless free expanse
Are flashing, confusion, rumbling, and thunder.
Sea glazed with turbid, lusterless gleaming,
How lovely you are in desolate night!

O swell of sea, O huge sea swell,
Whose holiday do you celebrate so?
The waves scud on, with grumbling, sparkling,
While delicate stars gaze down from heights.

Amid this heaving, amid this gleaming,
I stand all lost, as though in dreams.
O how so fain am I to drown
My soul entire in their enchantment.

When souls are not at peace with God,
However they loving suffer,
They will not reach to joy, alas,
But only themselves will test.

O soul which wholly was devoted
To a single, holy love,

Who breathed and ached for it alone,
The Lord's Grace be upon you!

His is the mercy and the power,
His is the warming ray,
The splendrous flower blooming in air,
And pure pearls in sea depths.

In the stillness of my martyrdom
Some times oppress me more than others.
Their grievous yoke, their fateful burden
My lines cannot convey nor bear.

All suddenly is chill. Foreign
To tears and pity, empty, dark,
The past does not waft gentle shades
But lies a corpse beneath the earth.

The world above it, sharp and real,
But without sunbeams, without love,
A world indifferent and soulless,
Has neither known nor now recalls her.

And I alone, made dull by grief,
I would bear witness, but cannot:
I am a broken skiff, wavethrown
Onto a wild and nameless shore.

O Lord, grant racking agony,
Dissolve the numbness of my soul:
You captured *her*, but memory's pang,
The poignant pang of her, leave me:

Of her, of her, who went her way
Unto the desperate struggle's end,
So ardent, so fervid was her love
In all despite of men and fate;

Of her, of her, who could not vanquish
Her fate, but would not be conquered herself;
Of her, of her, who knew till death
How to suffer, pray, believe, and love.

Est in arundineis modulatio musica ripis[93] 𝕾

> There is a melody in seawaves,
> A concord in elements' quarrels,
> And a mellifluous musical rustling
> Runs streaming in rippling rushes.
>
> There is a steady system in all,
> Full consonance in nature;
> It is only in our phantom freedom
> That we sense discord with her.
>
> Whence and how has discord arisen?
> Why does the soul not sing
> In choir with the sea, why does
> This thinking reed complain?

TO MY FRIEND YA. P. POLONSKY[94] 𝕾

> No more the vibrant tone of your sweet voice,
> Mute night about me that will have no morning:
> The last sparse smoke, elusive in the gloom,
> Flies quickly from the now extinguished fire.

𝕾

> Today, my friend, marks fifteen years[95]
> From that blissful, fatal day
> When she gave over all her soul,
> Abandoned herself to me.
>
> This year, without reproach nor plaint,[96]
> All lost, I greet my fate:

[93] There is a musical modulation in the reeds of the shore. The epigraph is taken from a poem of the fourth-century Roman poet Ausonius.
[94] Polonsky, a minor poet, was a friend of Tyutchev's and a colleague on the Committee of Foreign Censorship.
[95] The addressee is unknown, but the "she" of the poem is probably Deniseva.
[96] The poem was probably written in July 1865, almost a year after Deniseva's death.

As dreadful loneliness 'til death
As loneliness entombed.

ON THE EVE OF THE FIRST ANNIVERSARY OF AUGUST 4, 1864[97] 🕊

I wander now along the highway
In the quiet light of dying day.
I am grown weary, my legs are sinking.
Dear love, O do you see me?

It is grown darker, darker on earth,
The last reflection of day has flown.
This is the world where you and I lived.
My angel, do you see me?

Tomorrow we will pray and weep,
Tomorrow recalls that fatal day.
My angel, wherever souls may soar,
My angel, do you see me?

🕊

How suddenly and brightly,
In transitory glory,
The aerial arch arose
In the moist bluetinted sky!
One end plunged in the woods,
The other behind a cloud;
It girded half the sky
And faded in the heights.

O how the eyes are pleasured
To see this rainbow vision!
We have it but a moment,
So catch it, catch it quickly!
See there—it pales already.
One minute, two—and then?

[97] The "1864" refers to the year of Deniseva's death. The poem was written in 1865.

Gone, as will go entirely
The world you breathe and live.

❧

The sky of night is louring,
In all its ends beclouded.
There is no threat, there is no thought—
A dull, a desolate dream.
But fiery flaming summer lightnings,
Igniting one another,
Hold conversation among themselves
Like demons deaf and dumb.

As though upon appointed signal,
A strip of sky lights up,
And fields and distant woods stand out
An instant from the gloom.
And then again is all grown dark,
All calm in delicate darkness,
As though there were some secret matter
On high there being decided.

❧

No day the soul was free from aching,
Pining for the past,
It sought the Word, it did not find,
It yearned, yearned every day,

Like one who grieves, in anguish burning,
Grieves for his native land,
And on a sudden learns one day
Seawaves have covered it.

❧

However gossip might run wild,[98]
However it gnawed at her,

[98] Apparently addressed to one Nadezhda A. Akinfieva, who had been
divorced and became, therefore, the subject of scandal.

The honest candor of her eyes
Was stronger than any demon.

So frank and amiable was she,
So good were all her acts,
The azure of her cloudless soul
Remained all unabashed.

No trace of silly calumny
Or gossip worried her;
And even slander never rumpled
Her airy, silken curls.

Reflections of golden roofs[99]
Flow slowly in the lake.
A host of ancient fame
Beholds itself in the lake.
Life plays, the sun is warming,
But under both of them
The past here wondrously wafts
A magic all its own.

The golden sun is shining,
The flowing lake is flashing.
The grandeur of the past
Here breathes as though in slumber;
It dozes sweetly, heedless,
Untroubled by vivid dreams
Or ephemeral alarms
Of voices of the swans.

When our declining powers begin
To violate our trust,
And we, like men who've lived too long,
Must yield to new-come strangers,

[99] Probably written during the summer of 1866, when Tyutchev made a visit to Tsarskoe Selo.

O then, good genius, may you save us
From mean and scurvy sneers,
From calumnies, from venting bile
Against a life betrayed;

From sentiments of smoldering malice
Against a world renewed
Where new and youthful guests now sit
At feasts prepared for them;

From bitter bile of recognition
That the stream no longer bears us,
That others now are being called,
That others have been summoned;

From all those passionate feelings hidden
So deeply for so long:
They are the fractious senile fervor
Of shameful senile love.

However grievous our final hour—
That weariness of mortal pain
We cannot understand—
More dire yet is it for souls
To watch as their best memories
Become extinct within them.

Again I stand before the Neva,
Anew, as in years past,
I look, as though I were alive,
Into these dozing waters.

There are no lights in the bluestained sky,
All calm in white enchantment;
Along the pensive Neva alone
The lunar aureole streams.

Is this a dream I dream in sleep
Or do I really see

What we together by moonlight saw
When we were still alive?

FIRES[100] 🕊

Spread wide and boundless,
An endless threatening cloud,
Smoke after smoke, smoke chasms
Hang over earth.

Dead shrubs lie strewn,
Grass smolders, does not flame,
A row of burned-out firs
Is on the skyline.

No sparks, just smoke
At fire's sorrowful site.
Where is the evil destroyer,
The master almighty?

But here and there,
By stealth, like some red beast
That creeps through bushes, the fire
Living runs.

When twilight advances,
The smoke blends with the dark.
Now regimental fires
Light up its camp.

Man stands despondent,
In silence, his courage lost
Before this hostile power,
A helpless child.

🕊

Clouds shelter in the sky,
And radiant in the heat,

---

[100] There were some bad forest fires near Petersburg in the summer of 1868.

The river sparkling rolls,
A mirror made of steel.

The heat grew ever stronger,
A shadow slipped to the mute
Tree grove and wafted a scent
Of honey from the whitening fields.

A gorgeous day! Ages
Will pass, in eternal order
The river will flow and sparkle
And fields will breathe in the heat.

It was not granted to us to foresee
What answer our words would meet.
To us compassion rather is granted,
As to us granted is grace.

There are two powers, two fateful powers;
Our lives are in their hands
From cradle days unto the grave—
Death and human Law.

They both are irresistible;
Accountable to none,
They grant no quarter, plaints ignore,
Their sentence seals all lips.

More honest Death. Alien to bias,
Unmoved and uncorrupted
By either meek or grumbling brothers,
She scything equals all.

The world is not so: a jealous master,
He suffers no struggle nor discord,
He mows not closely but often rips
The best stem from the root.

Death grieves—alas, a double grief—
When young and prideful strength

Engages in biased battle, firm
Of gaze, a smile on lips,

And she, in fateful awareness of all
Her rights, in beauty bold,
Undaunted, somehow enchanting, goes forth
To meet man's calumnies.

No mask has she to screen her brow,
Her brow may not be humbled.
She shakes threats, railing, and raging blame
Like dust from her youthful curls.

She grieves: the greater her innocence,
The guiltier she seems.
Not so the world: She is more inhumane
The more humanly candid the fault.

೮

Nature is a sphinx. Indeed,
Her testing undoes man the more,
Perhaps because she never had,
Nor yet has now, a riddle at all.

೮

Let not our separation depress us,
Let us submit to it:
Another torment awaits the heart,
More onerous and painful.

The season of separation has passed,
And in our hands remains
No more than but a covering
Diaphanous to our sight.

We know: beneath this gauzy cloth
Is all that pains the soul,
A kind of strange invisible being
Concealed from us, and silent.

What is the purpose of such temptations?
The soul, perforce confused,

Is in a puzzling circle whirled
Reluctantly about.

The season of separation has passed,
We do not dare, in time,
To seize and rip apart the veil,
So odious is it to us!

TO JULIA F. ABAZA[101] 🖎

'Tis true—harmonious instruments' power
Will hold a soul in thrall,
And every man alive does love
His dark but native tongue.

There is a plaint in it, a pulsing,
As though it were a spirit
In chains imprisoned begging freedom
And striving to speak aloud.

There is no trace of this in your singing;
It is not this we feel.
There is complete deliverance,
An end to prison and struggle.

Escaped from out its vale of tears,
With all its shackles cut,
This soul that is delivered exults
In liberty entire.

The dark is lifted from the world[102]
By this almighty call;
We hear not sounds, but *a living soul*,
We hear your soul in them.

TO K. B.[103] 🖎

I met you, and all the past
Revived in my dying heart;

[101] Julia Abaza was a musician and singer of the time. A friend of Gounod
and Liszt, she was quite important in Russian musical circles.

[102] The word Tyutchev uses here is *svet*, which can mean both "world"
and "light."

[103] Written in 1870 to the Baroness Krudner, whom Tyutchev had first

I remembered a golden time,
And my heart was so warm.

As there are days, as there are hours
In the season of late fall,
When touches of spring begin to blow
And something awakes in us,

So blown on by the breath of those years
Of inner plenitude,
With rapture forgotten long ago
I look at your dear features.

I gaze at you as though in dreaming,
As after parting eternal.
Those sounds I knew are louder now,
No longer silent in me.

It is not just remembrance now,
Now life speaks out anew,
Here are the selfsame charms in you,
The same love in my soul.

O brother, after so many years with me[104]
You went where all of us will go;
I stand alone now on the naked height,
And emptiness is all around.

How long will I stand here alone? A day,
Another year, and emptiness
Where I am now, beholding the darkness of night,
And what I am now I do not know.

No trace is left, how easy not to be!
With or without me—what does it matter?
It will all be the same: the same blizzard howling,
Same darkness, same encircling steppe.

---

met in Karlsbad.
[104] Written in late December 1870 to Tyutchev's brother, Nikolai Ivanovich, who had died on December 8, 1870.

My course is run, uncounted is the waste,
A living life is far behind me,
There is no going on; most certainly
I stand now in the fatal queue.

&

Of that life of yours which once stormed here,[105]
Of that blood of yours which river-ran here,
What now survives, what reaches us?
A barrow or two may be seen today.

An oak or two has grown on them,
And spread its branches wide and bold.
They preen, they rustle, and do not care
Whose ashes, whose memories their roots invade.

It seems that nature knows no past,
Our spectral years are alien to her,
And faced with her we dimly feel
That we are only nature's dream.

She greets in turn each child of hers
Who has fulfilled his futile task,
And hails each equally to her
Omnivorous abyss of peace.

&

A punishing God has deprived me of all,[106]
Health, strength of will, my breath, and sleep.
He has left only you to me,
So that I still may pray to Him.

---

[105] Written in 1871, as a result of a trip to the town of Vshchizh, near which were some ancient barrows.
[106] Written in 1873 during Tyutchev's last illness and dedicated to his wife.

THE
POLITICAL
POEMS

TO PUSHKIN'S ODE ON LIBERTY[1] ❧

Aflame with the fire of freedom
And stifling the clank of his chains,
Alceus' ghost waked in your lyre
And slavery's dust fell from it.
Sparks flashing spun from your lyre
And shooting far their stream,
Poor mimics of God's flame,
They fell on the brow of the Tsar.

Blesséd is he whose stern bold voice
Was chosen to utter holy truths
To hardened tyrants, their dignity
Forgot, their throne as well forgot.
You were awarded this great fate,
O nursling, pupil of the Muse!

With all the strength of your melodies
Touch deep, affect, and metamorphose
The frigid friends of autocracy
Into the friends of goodness and beauty!
But do not trouble citizens' peace,
Nor tarnish the luster of the crown.
O singer, may your magic chord
Assuage but not alarm the heart
Beneath imperial brocade!

DECEMBER 14, 1825[2] ❧

Autocracy perverted you,
Its sword did strike you down;
The Law, impartial, uncorrupted,
Confirmed this penalty.
The people, shunning perfidy,

---

[1] Tyutchev was only seventeen when he wrote this poem attacking Pushkin's celebrated ode, which had been composed in 1817. Tyutchev's political attitudes were already set, although this youthful work was not published until 1887. However, Tyutchev always admired Pushkin as a poet (see "January 29, 1837").

[2] Written in 1826 on the Decembrist revolt of the previous December 14.

Revile your very names,
Your memory is corpselike buried
Fore'er beneath the ground.

O sacrifices to mad ideas,
Perhaps it was your hope
That with your meager blood you'd melt
The everlasting pole.
But barely did it glitter, smoking,
On the ageless icy mass:
The breath of iron winter blew—
And not one trace remained.

OLEG'S SHIELD[3] 🙿

I

"O Allah! shed your light upon us!
O true believers' model and staff,
O hypocritical heretics' giaour!
     Your prophet, Mohammed!"

2

"O our fortress, O our rampart,
Great God! Lead us at this moment
As in the desert in ancient days
     You led your chosen people!"

Voiceless midnight! All is silent.
Just then the moon broke through the clouds,
And over the gates of Istamboul
     The shield of Oleg flashed.

THE ALPS[4] 🙿

The snowcapped Alps peer through
The azure twilight dusk;

[3] Written in late 1828 or early 1829 at the time of the Russo-Turkish War (one among many), won by the Russians. According to the *Primary Chronicle*, Kievan Prince Oleg's shield had been hung above the gates of Constantinople as a sign of his victory over the Greeks. Tyutchev is calling for a Russian Orthodox Constantinople, even though Oleg was a pagan who swore by Peroun, god of thunder, and by Volos, god of cattle.
[4] Written in 1830. A favorite theme of Tyutchev's was not only the

Their pale and deadened eyes
Strike with icy terror.
Bewitched by an unknown power,
By mists surrounded, awesome,
They dream 'til Dawn's ascent,
Like unto fallen Tsars!

The East but starts to glow,
Ending baneful spells;
The crown of the elder brother
Is first to light the sky;
From the greater brother's head
A beam runs to the lesser,
And all a risen family
Shines out of the gold in the crowns.

As Agamemnon sacrificed[5]
His daughter to the gods,
Imploring a propitious wind
From angry celestial spheres,[6]
So we at sad and grieving Warsaw
Have struck a fatal blow.
Yes, at this bloody price we buy
The safety and peace of Russia.[7]

But take from us the crown of shame
Enwoven by servile hands!
Not for autocracy's Koran
Did Russian blood flow free.
No! No hungry demons here
Inspired our sword to battle,

---

contrast between Russia and the West, but between the Slavs and the West
(the "family" of line 15). Pigarev does not think this is a political poem.

[5] Written in 1831.

[6] Literally, "from the angry heavens."

[7] The reference is to the investiture of Warsaw by the Russian army in
August 1831 in the course of the Polish revolt. Anti-Russian sentiment ran
high throughout Western Europe. (See A. Herzen, *My Life and Thoughts*,
IV, for a point of view opposed to that of Tyutchev.)

Nor Janissary's tamed cruelty,
Nor hangman's obedience.

Another thought, another faith
Did beat in Russian breasts:
To keep our nation safe by threat
Of this salutary example;
To gather kindred Slavic clans
Beneath the Russian banner
And teach them how to march in step
Together like an army.

A conscience of the highest order
Led on our valiant people.
It knows that Heav'n will justify
The path that it has taken.
It senses a star above its head
In reaches beyond its sight
And hastens pressing after the star
To a mysterious goal.

You whom the fraternal arrow pierced,
Fulfilling the verdict of fate,
You fell, an eagle of our clan,
On the purifying pyre.
Believe the word of the Russian people;
Your ashes will we keep sacred;
Our common freedom, like the Phoenix,
Will be reborn in them.

NAPOLEON[8]

I

Son of the Revolution, boldly did you
Fight with your dreaded mother, fighting you fell.
Your tyrannic genius did not vanquish her.
A battle impossible, a labor vain!
For still you carried her within yourself.

---

[8] Parts I and II of "Napoleon" were written in 1836, although separately, and Part III was written by 1850, possibly as early as 1840, the year that Napoleon's body was brought from St. Helena to Paris.

2

Two demons there were that served him,
Two powers that wondrously merged:
Eagles soared in his head,
Vipers writhed in his breast.
He boldly flew like an eagle
On ranging, inspired wings,
And with the serpent's cunning
Planned his daring assault.
But the consecrating power
Beyond his understanding
Did not illumine his soul,
Did not descend upon him.
Earth's, not God's, flame was he,
He sailed proud, scorning waves,
But faith's rock under the waters
Shattered his leaky boat.

3

And so you stood, with Russia before you.
Prophetic magus, foretelling battle,
You uttered the fatal words yourself:
"Now let her destiny be decided!"
Your incantation was not in vain:
Your voice had destiny's response.
But then in banishment you answered
The fatal reply with a rebus new.[9]

Years passed, and from your exile strait
Brought back a corpse to your native land,
To the river banks so dear to you,

Most Russians, and in particular the Slavophiles, held Napoleon—and France in general—in abhorrence in the nineteenth century. France was not only the nation that had invaded Russia in 1812 (and was to be, in Russian intellectual eyes, the major ally of Turkey against her in the Crimean War in 1854), it was also the bourgeois nation *par excellence*, a quality disliked by both Slavophiles and Westernizers. See, on this subject, Tolstoy's *War and Peace*, Gogol's *Selected Passages from Correspondence with Friends*, Dostoevsky's *Winter Notes on Summer Impressions*, and Herzen's *My Life and Thoughts*.

Tyutchev, in Part I, saw Napoleon as a product of the Revolution, which made him worse, in Tyutchev's eyes, than a simple invader. See below, "Russia and the Revolution."

[9] That is, Napoleon's escape from Elba.

A troubled spirit, you rest at last.
But sleep is light. At night awearied,
You sometimes rise and Eastward look;
At once confounded, you flee, as though
You scent the breeze preceding dawn.

TO HANKA[10] 🐾

Must we always live apart?
Is it not time to come
To our senses and give our hands
To all our kinsmen and friends?

For ages were we blind,
Like blind men begging we roamed,
We roved, and we were scattered
To all the ends of earth.

It happened on a time
That somehow we collided:
Blood more than once flowed free,
And swords tore kinsmen's breasts.

This senseless enmity's seed
Gave birth to hundredfold fruit,
And many the tribe that perished
Or vanished in foreign lands.

Unchristians, foreigners
Disjoined us, broke us apart:
Some's tongue the German defiled,
And others the Turk disgraced.

Then in this night of gloom,
Here on the heights of Prague,
A hero with modest hand
Enkindled a beacon in darkness.[11]

---

[10] Václar Hanka (1791–1861), a Czech, was a strong supporter of Czecho-Russian friendship who was well known to many Russian men-of-letters. Tyutchev met him in Prague in 1841, the year of the writing of this poem.

[11] In 1819, Hanka published the *Kraledvorsky Chronicle*, supposedly lyric and epic songs of the Czech nation. Later he admitted that he had written them himself on the basis of chronicles and legends. The important thing

O with what sudden rays
Was all the land illumined!
And all our Slavic earth
Exposed before our view!

Mountains, steppes, and shores
The splendid day lit clear,
From Neva to Montenegro,
From Carpathians to the Urals.

Dawn rises over Warsaw,
And Kiev has oped its eyes;
With Moscow's golden domes
The Kremlin began to speak.

Anew we understood
The sounds of brothers' names.
Grandsons will see as real
What fathers only dreamed.

POSTSCRIPT[12] 🐾

Thus did I call, thus say.
Now thirty years have passed:
More urgent is the labor,
The evil wider spread.

Just[13] man, O sainted shade
Now standing with the Lord,
Let your life be the pledge
Our yearned-for day will come.

For all your constancy
In the never-ending battle
Let this first *All-Slav* feast[14]
Now be our gift to you.

---

about the book, however, was its assertion of Czech nationality and Slavic
nature against the Germans. It was Hanka's Slavism that particularly appealed
to Tyutchev.

[12] This "Postscript" was written for the Slavic conference that took place
in Petersburg and Moscow from May 8 to 27, 1867. Eighty-one representatives from the Balkans and Western Europe attended.

[13] *Pravda* is used here.

[14] Literally, "Let this first celebration of *All-Slavdom*."

Which flatters popular wisdom more:[15]
The Babel of German unity
Or the crafty republican system
Of brawling French uproar?

SEA AND CLIFF[16]

It rises rebelling and seethes,
It slashes, whistles, and squalls,
It would leap up to stars,
Up to th' unshakable heights.
Is it hell, has hellish power
Laid out Gehenna's fire
Beneath the seething cauldron,
Has it reversed the deeps
And set them upside down?

With breakers of raging waves
The sea rollers ceaselessly beat,
With squall, whistle, scream, and howl,
Against the coastal cliff.
But calm and haughty, by whims
Of waves remaining unmoved,
Steadfast, immutable,
Old as the universe,
Our giant, still you stand!

Enfrenzied by the battle,
As though to final assault[17]
The howling waves anew
Swarm over your granite bulk.
But its roaring onslaught broken
By the immutable stone,
The shattered billow splashed back,

---

[15] Written in 1848 in reference to the German and French revolutionary concerns of that year. See below, "Russia and the Revolution."

[16] Written in 1848. The sea is a symbol of the revolutions in the West; the cliff, a symbol of Russia.

[17] Literally, "fateful assault." It seems better, however, to preserve Tyutchev's battle imagery.

And the enfeebled gush
Now streams a muddy foam.

So stand, O mighty cliff!
Wait but one hour, another—
The rolling wave will weary
Of battle with your heel.
With its evil game fatiguing,
It will subside anew.
And howling and battle over,
Beneath the giant's heel
The wave will stretch anew.

RUSSIAN GEOGRAPHY[18] 🙚

Moscow, Peter's city, and Constantine's city
Are the holy capitals of the Russian realm.
But where its outer limit, where its border,
To north, to east, to south, and where the sun sets?
Destiny will unmask them in future times.

Seven inland seas,[19] and seven great rivers,
From Nile to Neva, from Elbe to China, from Volga
To Euphrates, from the Ganges to the Danube—
That is the Russian realm. And never will
It pass, as the Spirit foresaw and Daniel predicted.[20]

DAWN[21] 🙚

The cock has crowed three times; its crowing
Is sharp and brisk and bold;
The skyborne moon has been extinguished;
The Bosphorus stream has reddened.

Still silent are the chimes of bells,
Though Dawn is flushing the East;

---

[18] Written in either 1848 or 1849.
[19] It is difficult to know precisely which seas Tyutchev had in mind. Certainly the Caspian, the Black, the Azov, the Mediterranean; possibly the Baltic, the Aral, and Lake Ladoga.
[20] See Daniel 11 :44.
[21] Written in late 1849, when Turkish-Russian tension was mounting, and published in 1854, the year the Crimean War broke out.

131

Protracted night has passed away,
And bright day quickly comes.

Arise, O Rus! The hour is near!
Arise to do Christ's service!
Is it not time, while crossing yourself,
To ring Byzantium's bells?

Now let the church bell sound ring out
And all the East resound!
It summons and awakens you—
Arise, take heart, to arms!

Enclothe your breast in the armor of faith,
And God be with you, stout giant!
O Rus, great is the coming day,
The worldwide, Orthodox day![22]

A PROPHECY[23] 🖎

It was not rumbling rumor in our people,
The news was not born in our generation.
An ancient lofty voice pronounced it:
"The fourth of the ages already is closing;
It is coming true; the hour is striking!"[24]

When Byzantium is restored to us
The ancient vaults of Saint Sophia
Will shelter the altar of Christ anew.[25]
Kneel then before it, O Tsar of Russia—
You will arise all Slavdom's Tsar![26]

---

[22] Many Russians saw the Crimean War as a Holy War being waged to free their Orthodox Slavic brothers from Turkish Mohammedan domination.

[23] Written in 1850. Tyutchev was all in favor of a war with Turkey, which he was convinced would result in Russian—and Slavic—glory.

[24] The Turks took Byzantium almost exactly 500 years earlier.

[25] The Cathedral of St. Sophia was turned into a mosque when Byzantium fell. It is still a mosque.

[26] The tsar, Nicholas I, underlined the last two lines of this poem and wrote in the margin: "Phrases like this are not permissible."

It is three years that tongues have raved.[27]
Now it is spring, and every spring,
Like flocking birds before a storm,
More anxious the din, cacaphony greater.

Princes and powers in grave distress
Hold to the reins with trembling hands,
The mind is choked by ominous pangs,
Popular fancies, sick, savage dreams.

But *God is with us!* Gone mad, in storm
And gloom, from up the bottom sweeping,
The depths dashed rashly over us.

But never did your gaze grow dim!
The wind raged. But "It shall not be so!"
And at your word[28] the wave rushed back.

O no, my dwarf, my coward unequalled![29]
However mean and craven
You be, your soul of little faith
Will not tempt holy Rus.

Will she renounce her holy hopes,
All her persuasion's needs,
Will she upon a sudden renounce
Her calling just for you?

Are you so dear to Providence,
So friendly, so at one
With it that, valuing your sloth,
It suddenly will stop?

[27] Written in 1850, the poem is concerned with the revolutions of 1848.
[28] The phrase is quoted from the manifesto published by Nicholas I on March 14, 1848.
[29] Written in 1850, the poem is addressed to Count Nesselrode, Russian minister of foreign affairs from 1816 to 1856. He had been Alexander I's representative at the Congress of Vienna in 1815. At the time that Tyutchev was writing, Nesselrode was following a more or less pro-Austrian policy, a policy of which Tyutchev, as a pan-Slavist, could not approve.

The dwarf of line 1 is a pun in Russian. The Russian word for dwarf is *karlik*. Nesselrode's first name was Karl.

Trust not in holy Rus who will,
But let her trust herself.
The Lord will not defer her triumph
To please men's cowardice.

What once was promised by the fates
Belonged to her in the cradle,
What was bequeathed by centuries
And faith of all her Tsars,

What once the followers of Oleg
Went forth with swords to conquer,
What Catherine's double-headed eagle
Once sheltered with its wing—

No, you will not rob us of scepter
And crown of Byzantium.
The universal fate of Russia,
No, you will not usurp!

The order we have longed for will be[30]
In total triumph at last established
In all the mass of this world's Slavs
When Poland with Russia is reconciled,
And these two will be reconciled
Not in Petersburg nor Moscow,
But rather in Kiev and Constantinople.[31]

THE NIEMAN[32]

Is this you, stately, grand Nieman?
Is this indeed your stream before me?
How many years and with what glory
Have you been Russia's faithful guard!

[30] Written in 1850.
[31] Because, in Tyutchev's view, Kiev is the old Slavic capital and Constantinople is the Orthodox one.
[32] Written in 1853, when Tyutchev stopped in Kovno (changed to Kaunas when it became the capital of Lithuania) on his way to Petersburg from abroad. For the Lithuanians the river was the Memel rather than the Nieman.

Once only, bending to God's will,
Did you allow the foe within.[33]
For centuries did you preserve
The safety of our Russia's threshold.

Do you recall the past, Nieman,
The moment of that fateful year
When he was standing up above you—
Yes, he, that mighty southern demon—[34]
And you flowed past as you do now,
Beneath the enemy bridges roaring,
While he with his amazing eyes
Looked tenderly upon your stream?

Triumphantly his regiments
Advanced, their banners gaily flapping,
Their bayonets glittered in the sun,
The bridges rumbled beneath their guns,
And from his height, as though some god,
It seemed, he hovered over them
And set all things in motion, surveyed
It all with his amazing eyes.

One thing alone he did not see:
This glorious warrior did not see
That there, on the opposing side,
Another stood, stood and waited.
His host marched past, each one of them
In martial bearing dread. Yet then
The ineluctable right hand
Of God had set its seal upon them.

Triumphantly his regiments
Advanced, their banners proudly fluttered,
Their bayonets streamed lightning flashes,
Their drumbeats sounded far and wide.
Their number was without an end,
And out of all their endless rank

---

[33] The French captured Kovno, which is on the Nieman, in 1812.
[34] Napoleon. "Southern" more because of his Corsican birth than his French nationality.

135

The number of but one in ten
Escaped the fatal brand of shame.[35]

A SPIRITUAL PROPHECY[36] 🙙

Days of battle and triumph will come,
Rus will achieve her heirdom's borders,
Old Moscow will become
The *newest* capital of her three.[37]

🙙

You are not now concerned with rhymes,[38]
O native Russian Word!
The crop is ripe, the reaper ready,
An exalted time has come.

The lie has been embodied in steel;
By some divine allowance
Not all the world, but all of hell
Now threats your overthrow.

Now all profane blaspheming minds,
All peoples loathed by God
Have risen from the dark realm's depths
Proclaiming light and freedom![39]

They ready prisonment for you,
Predict disgrace for you,
You, word and life, illuminer
Of better times to come!

O in this stern severe ordeal,[40]
In this last fateful battle,

---

[35] Only about 50,000 men of Napoleon's *Grande Armée* of approximately 500,000 returned from the Russian adventure.

[36] Written in late 1853 or early 1854, on the eve of the Crimean War.

[37] The other two for Tyutchev would be Kiev and Constantinople.

[38] Written in late 1854, after the start of the Crimean War.

[39] A reference to France, England, and Piedmont, the three Western enemies of Russia in the war.

[40] Literally, "O in this stern [or severe] ordeal." I have used both adjectives where Tyutchev uses only one for rhythmic reasons.

Be ever faithful to yourself,
And justified to God.[41]

≈

These villages so poor,[42]
This meager, barren nature:
My native, suffering land,
The Russian people's land!

Proud eyes of foreigners
Will never grasp nor note
The inner light beneath
Your humble nakedness.

Crushed by the cross's burden,
The Heavenly Tsar has traveled
In servile guise across you,
My native land, with blessing.

≈

Here from one sea unto a sea[43]
The telegraphic line glides;[44]
Much glory and much grief this line
From time to time recites.

The traveler tracking with his eyes
Remarks how now and then
Prophetic birds sit down to roost
In order along the line.

See from the glades an ebon raven
Swooped up to perch on it,
Perched there and cawed and waved its wings,
In gayness ever growing.

---

[41] Literally, "Justified before [or in the sight of] God."

[42] Written in mid-1855. Dostoevsky quoted this poem in "The Grand Inquisitor" chapter of *The Brothers Karamazov*.

[43] Written in August 1855, before the fall of Sebastopol to the allied forces, but the situation was daily growing worse for the Russians.

[44] From the Black Sea to the Baltic.

137

It shrieks on high and loud exults,
And gyrates wide above it:
Is it blood that the raven scents
In news of Sebastopol?

ON THE OCCASION OF THE COMING OF THE AUSTRIAN ARCHDUKE TO THE BURIAL OF NICHOLAS[45] ❧

No! There are limits to our patience
And bounds to impudence!
I swear my oath to his crowned shade,
We will not bear it all!

Now everywhere a common call
Of anguished sorrow bursts:
Away, away, O Austrian Judas,
Away from his coffin's lid!

Away with their betraying kiss![46]
Their apostolic breed[47]
May all be branded with one name:
Judas Iscariot!

❧

It was not God you served, nor Russia,[48]
You served yourself alone,
And all your deeds, both good and evil,
All was a lie in you, but empty ghosts:
You were not Tsar, but acting sham.

[45] Written in March 1855. The archduke came to the funeral of Nicholas I on February 17, 1855 (Nicholas died January 18, 1855).
[46] Many Russians thought Austria was betraying them by following a policy of neutrality in the Crimean War instead of joining the Russian side as had been expected.
[47] The Austrian emperor was officially his "Apostolic Majesty."
[48] Addressed to the dead Tsar Nicholas I, this poem was probably written in the late summer or early fall of 1855. It was not printed until 1922, for obvious reasons. The poem represents a sharp about-face in Tyutchev's feelings for the tsar, probably occasioned by the increasingly obvious failure of Nicholas' policies, particularly in the Crimea.

1856[49] 🪶

Blind we stand before our fate,
Not ours to tear the veil from it.
Not I do I disclose to you,
But rather prophetic spirits' ravings.

The end is still far distant from us:
The thunder rages, the thunder grows,
Now in an iron cradle we see
The New Year born in peals of thunder.

Its features are with horror grim,
Blood on its hands and on its brow.
But not alone alarms of war
Does it bring men on earth below.

Not just a warrior will it be,
But zealous tool of God's requital,
And, late avenger, will achieve
The blow that has so long been planned.

For battle and retribution sent,
It brings two blades along with it:
The one is combat's bloody sword,
The other the hangman's gibbet axe.

For whom, however? One neck alone
Or is the entire people doomed?
The fateful words are indistinct,
And vague the sleep beyond the grave.[50]

---

[49] Written on December 31, 1855, according to the manuscript title, although a contemporary of Tyutchev's, P. I. Bertenev, claimed to have heard it some time at the beginning of 1855. The content of the poem makes the December 31, 1855, date more likely, since it clearly shows Tyutchev's gloom at the fast approaching defeat of Russia in the Crimean War, a defeat which did in fact come about in 1856.

[50] Some commentators have thought that Tyutchev really was referring to spiritualism in this poem. We do know that he was interested in the subject at this time. Certainly, a spiritualist interpretation would clarify—if spiritualism is clarification—the first and last stanzas.

TO ALEXANDER II[51] 🐚

You seized your day. From ages marked
For blessing by the Lord Almighty,
He removed the slavish shape from man,
Made one again the family.[52]

🐚

A horrid dream did burden us,[53]
A horrid, monstrous dream:
We wade in blood, we battle corpses
Arisen for burial new.

Intrepid passion, treason, lying,
Thieves in the house of prayer[54]
With crucifix and knife in hand[55]
This eighth month drag these battles.

The whole world, as though drunk with lying,
All shapes and shifts of evil!
No, never so boldly has human falsehood
Called forth God's truth to battle!

This cry of blind compassion, worldwide
Cry to rabid battle,
Debauched minds and distorted words,[56]
All risen, all threaten you,

O native land! Such general levy
The world has never seen.
Great is your import, Rus! Take heart,
Stand firm, and overcome!

---

[51] Written in March 1861. Alexander had published the decree liberating the serfs the previous January.

[52] Literally, "And restored the younger brother to the family."

[53] Written in August 1863. Tyutchev is attacking the diplomatic activities of Austria, England, and France in support of the Polish uprising. The uprising, suppressed by the Russians, aroused great sympathy throughout Europe.

[54] Literally, "A den of thieves in the house of prayer."

[55] A reference to the Roman Catholicism of Poland.

[56] That is, the sympathy of Western Europe for the Poles.

THE ENCYCLICAL[57] 🖎

One day the hammer of the Lord of Truth
Cast down and crushed the Hebrew temple,[58]
And by his own sword slaughtered, the High Priest
Within it drew his final breath.

More frightfully and more implacably
In our days—days when God is judging—
Will execution be done in Apostate Rome
Upon the pseudo-vicar of Christ.

He has been much forgiven in past ages—
His crooked talk and his dark deeds—
The God of Truth and Justice[59] now, however,
Will not forgive his latest sin.

He will not perish by an earthly sword
Whose earthly sword has ruled so long;
His fateful words will rather cause his death:
"Freedom of conscience is but raving!"

TO PRINCE GORCHAKOV[60] 🖎

A fateful calling has fallen to you,
But he who called you watches.[61]
All best in Russia, all things alive
Observe you, trust you, wait.

Deceived insulted Russia's honor
You saved—no higher service.[62]
Now other deeds await you: defend
Her thought, her spirit save.[63]

[57] Written in 1864 in connection with the encyclical of Pope Pius IX
censuring freedom of conscience.

[58] Literally, "the Old Testament temple."

[59] In the original it is the God of *pravda*.

[60] Probably written in 1864. In 1856, Gorchakov had become minister
of foreign affairs, replacing Nesselrode. Tyutchev was well acquainted with
him. Indeed, he addressed his "Letter on the Censorship in Russia" (see
below) to Gorchakov.

[61] That is, Alexander II.

[62] A reference to Gorchakov's diplomatic activity during the Polish uprising.

[63] Probably a reference to the possibility of new repressive measures
which the government was contemplating at the time, particularly in regard
to censorship. (See below, "A Letter on the Censorship in Russia.")

He has been saved! It could not otherwise be![64]
A sense of joy flowed through all Russia.
But 'mid the prayers and 'mid the thankful tears
An urgent thought gnawed at the heart:

It is as though this shot did shame us all,
And never will this shame find exit.
It lies, alas, it lies a disgraceful stain
On all the history of the Russian people.

The East is silent, uncertain,[65]
A watchful silence throughout.
Is it sleep or expectation,
Day nearing or far away?
The peaks are faintly whitening,
Woods, dales are still in shadow,
Towns sleep and hamlets dream,
But raise your eyes to the sky.

See there: a streak appears;
As if glowing with hidden passion,
Its dazzle grows ever brighter.
Now she begins to flame,
And soon throughout the ether
Boundless a universal
Chiming of bells will peal
The conquering rays of the sun.

TO PRINCE SUVOROV[66]

In you are united
Two disparate trends:

[64] The poem was apparently written on the same day as D. V. Karakozov's attempted assassination of Alexander II, April 4, 1866.

[65] Probably written in 1865. The poem is a good example of Tyutchev's assimilation of his natural interests with his political ones.

[66] Probably written in early 1866, to Minister of War Alexander Arkadevich Suvorov, who seemed to be following a liberal policy. The poem was occasioned by Suvorov's refusal to welcome the governor general of

Devoutless devotion
And witless buffooning.

It seems that nature
Arranged you and doomed you
To action accountless
And speech without sequel.[67]

🔊

O will you long remain concealed[68]
In mist, O Russian star,
Or will you once for all unmask
This optical illusion?

Can it be that for eager eyes
That nightly yearn for you
A hollow deceitful meteor
Disperses and scatters your rays?

The gloom grows thicker, grief grows greater,
More certain is disaster.
See whose flag sinks there in the sea.
Awaken, now or never!

🔊

Despite her passing from the face of earth,[69]
The Tsar's soul still provides Truth[70] shelter.
Has anyone not heard the solemn word?
From age to age is it transmitted.

And now? Alas! What is it that we see?
Who shelters, holds the guest divine?

Siberia, M. N. Muravev, who had been responsible for the suppression of
the Polish rising of 1863–64.
  [67] Literally, "To irresponsible action, / To unpunished speech."
  [68] Written in 1866, in reference to the Cretan uprising against Turkey.
Tyutchev was hoping that Russia would come to the aid of the Cretan rebels
and at the same time settle its account with Turkey.
  [69] Written in 1866. Tyutchev is again concerned with the uprising in
Crete and calling for Russian intervention. He is probably making use of
the ancient legend of Astreae in the first line.
  [70] *Pravda.*

A lie, an evil lie all minds has rotted,
And all the world is Lie incarnate!

Again the East is reeking with fresh blood,
Again the carnage, howling and weeping,
Anew the feasting butcher of men's rights,
And victims given o'er to slander![71]

This age, this age revolts have educated,
Without a soul, with malevolent mind,
In city squares, in chambers, and at altars
Is everywhere Truth's personal foe.

But still a single powerful shelter remains,
A single holy altar for Truth:
It is in your soul, O our Orthodox Tsar,
Our benevolent, honest Russian Tsar!

᠊᠊᠊

Not by the mind is Russia understood,[72]
Nor is she measured by a common rule:
She has a special stature of her own;
In Russia one can only put his faith.[73]

SMOKE[74] ᠊᠊᠊

Upon a time here, mighty, lovely,
A charmed wood droned and greened,
Not wood, but all a varied world
Of visions and miracles.

---

[71] Supposedly Lady Buchanan, wife of the British ambassador to Petersburg, had called the Orthodox of Crete "cretins" instead of "Christians." The words are just as close in French, the language in which she supposedly made the remark ("crétins" and "chrétiens") and almost as close in Russian ("kretinov" and "khristiane").

[72] Written in November 1866.

[73] Or "One can only believe [have faith] in Russia"; or "Russia can only be believed in"; or "It is possible only to believe [have faith] in Russia."

[74] Written in 1867 apropos Turgenev's novel *Smoke*. Tyutchev contrasts this work of Turgenev, which paints a rather satiric picture of Russians abroad, with Turgenev's early work, especially *A Huntsman's Sketches*, published in 1852. Tyutchev liked *A Huntsman's Sketches* very much.

Rays filtered through and shadows quivered;
Birds racketed in the trees;[75]
Fleetfooted deer flashed in the thicket;
At times a hunter's horn blew.

At turnings a flock of familiar faces
In ripples of lovely light
With welcoming speeches flew to us
From out the shadowy wood.

What life, what fascination, this bright
And glorious feast for senses!
Though it pictured unearthly beings, this world
Of wonder was close to us.

Now with our former love again
We neared the secret wood.
Where is it? Who has drawn the curtain
Between the sky and earth?

What is this? What specter, what witchery?
Where are we? May eyes be trusted?
No more than smoke here, fifth element,
Smoke, bitter, endless smoke!

Occasional misshapen tree stumps
Jut from the ashy ground,
White fires with ominous crackling run
Along the blackburned branches.

No! This is dreaming. A wind will blow,
Dispersing the smoky ghost.
And then our wood will green again,
That magic wood of ours.

"The Fatherland's smoke is sweet and pleases us!"[76]
Is what the past poetic age does say.
But now a gifted writer seeks spots on the sun,
And smuts the Fatherland with stinking smoke!

[75] Literally, "Avian din did not fall silent in the trees."
[76] Also written in 1867 apropos Turgenev's novel *Smoke*. One remembers,

TO THE SLAVS[77] 🙵

A hearty welcome to you, brothers
Who come from all the Slavic lands,
Our welcome to every one of you,
The family feast is spread for all!
For reason did Russia summon you
Unto this fête of peace and love;
But know, dear guests, you are not here
As guests—you are among your own.

You are at home here, more at home
Than you were in your native lands,
Here where unknown is domination
Of rulers who speak in foreign tongues,
Here where the tongue of ruler and subject
Is one alone and one for all,
And Slavic birth is not esteemed
To be the weight of original sin![78]

Although we long were kept apart
By an inimical destiny,
Still we remain a single people,
The offspring of a single mother;
Still all of us are brothers born.
That, that is what they hate in us!
Russia is not forgiven you,
And you are not forgiven Russia.

They are confounded, frightened, indeed,
That all the Slavic family
In sight of enemy and friend
The first time utters, This is I!
Before the haunting memory
Of the stretching chain of wicked wrongs

---

of course, that Turgenev was a great admirer of Tyutchev's poetry. Indeed, he edited the first collection of Tyutchev's poems in 1854.

[77] Written in May 1867 for a Slavic conference in Petersburg and read at a banquet welcoming the Slavic guests on May 12. Cf. above, "To Hanka" and below, "To the Slavs."

[78] At the time, Russia was just about the only independent Slavic country. The others were mostly under the domination of Austria and Turkey.

This self-awareness of the Slavs,
Like God's chastisement, terrifies them.

Long since on European soil,
Where lies so pompously were sown,
Long since a Pharisaic science
Created two separate versions of truth:[79]
For them the law and equal rights,
For us coërcion and deceit,
And ancientness did strengthen them
As all your Slavic legacy.

What has endured for centuries
Is not exhausted, still is here,
Its weight still presses down upon us,
Upon us, we who gather here.
All of contemporary time
Is of these ancient ills still ill.
Kosovo Field is still untouched,[80]
White Mountain still has not been razed.[81]

Among our people—no little shame—
In all our kindred Slavic midst,
The only one who has escaped
Disgrace by them, has not incurred
Their enmity, is he who always
Has been their Judas everywhere:
They render honor to no man
Except their Judas with their kiss.[82]

Disgracefully peace-seeking tribe,
When will you be one with our people?
When will the time come to abolish

[79] Literally, "created double truth [*pravda*]."

[80] Kosovo Field is the site of the battle between the Turks and the Serbs in 1389. Obviously, the Turks won.

[81] White Mountain is a height near Prague where the Austro-Hungarian Emperor Ferdinand II defeated the Czechs in 1620, a defeat which led to the absorption of Bohemia into the Austro-Hungarian Empire.

[82] This and the following stanza express the view of Tyutchev as a pan-Slavist Orthodox of Western, Roman Catholic Poland. The Poles had not been invited to the conference; indeed, there were several demonstrations against them.

Your enmity and your distress,
When will the call to unity
Resound and what divides us crumble?
We wait and trust the prophecy—
Its day and hour is still unknown.[83]

And this faith in the truth of God
Will never die within our breasts,
Although we see much sacrifice
And much affliction still before us.
He lives, our sovereign who works all,
His tribunal still has not declined,
The words *The Tsar-Emancipator*
Will pass beyond the Russian border.

TO THE SLAVS[84]

*Man muss die Slaven an die
Mauer drücken*

They shriek, they roar, they loudly threaten:
"The Slavs will we press to the wall!"
As though it will not stop them short
In all the fever of their charge!

There is a wall, a solid wall—
It is no labor to press you to it.
But then what will that profit them?
That, that is labor to divine.

Dismaying is that wall's resilience,
At very least a granite cliff,[85]
A sixth part of the sphere of earth
Has it since long ago encircled.

They have attacked her more than once,
And once they ripped three stones from her;

---

[83] See above, "Russian Geography."

[84] Also written for the Slavic conference and read at a banquet on May 21. The epigraph "the Slavs must be pressed to the wall," is quoted from a statement made by the Austrian minister of foreign affairs at the time, Count von Beest, who was speaking of the Slavs within the Austro-Hungarian Empire.

[85] See above, "The Sea and the Cliff."

But then at last they did retreat
And broken were their knightly brows.[86]

She stands still now as then she stood,
The battle from her fortress watching.
It is not that she threatens now,
But all her stones are on alert.

So let the Germans' rabid rush
Drive forward and press you back
Unto her loopholes, bolts and bars—
And we will see what they receive!

However may the blind foe rave,
However their storm may menace you,
This uterine[87] wall will not betray you,
She never will reject her own.

She will ope passageways before you
And like a living citadel
Between you and the foe will stand
And always nearer him will draw.

A labor vain—no, you will never teach them:[88]
The more liberal, the more banal they are.
Civilization is a fetish for them,
But its idea they never will attain.

However you abase yourselves before her,
You never will find favor in Europe's sight:
In her opinion you will always be
Not servants of enlightenment, but serfs.

Deserved chastisement will be done[89]
For grievous sin, millenial sin.

---

[86] A reference to the Swedes and to the Livonian Knights of the Sword, who were defeated by Alexander Nevsky in 1240 and 1242, respectively.

[87] Literally, "native." "Uterine," however, seems to fit the poem's imagery better.

[88] Written in May 1867. Exactly what occasioned the poem is not known; but its content makes it sufficiently clear.

[89] Written in October 1867, the poem is concerned with Garibaldi's

He will not ward nor dodge the blow,
And God's Truth[90] will be clear to all.

Call not for any aid to check[91]
The just chastisement of God's truth,
Law will be done, the Popes' tiara
For the last time will bathe in blood.

And you,[92] who rightfully possess it,[93]
May the Lord save you and make you sage.
Now pray to Him, that your grey hairs
Be not defiled by shedding blood.

ON READING THE DISPATCHES OF THE IMPERIAL CABINET, PRINTED IN THE "JOURNAL DE ST. PETERSBURG"[94]

When man is finally redeemed
And the East is illumined anew,
The import of these splendid lines
Will then be understood.

Yes, then the dawn's first dazzling ray
Will touch and kindle them
And it will these prophetic pages
Enrich and sanctify.

The tears of the tribes grateful for freedom,
As the peoples' feelings flow,
Will gleaming glitter over them
Like God's immaculate dew.

---

campaign in the Papal States.

[90] *Pravda.*

[91] A reference to the pope's appeal to Napoleon III for help. The French did intervene and, in November 1867, stopped Garibaldi's advance.

[92] Pius IX, who occupied the papal throne at the time.

[93] That is, the tiara.

[94] Written in December 1867. The poem was occasioned by the publication of Russian diplomatic notes on the "Eastern question." In these notes the Russian government refused to guarantee the further integrity of the Turkish Empire.

Tyutchev hoped that this declaration would lead to an uprising of the Slavs within the Turkish dominions. The uprising did not take place.

On them is written all the tale
Both of what was and is;
The conscience of Europe has been bared
And Russia's honor saved!

*҈

Although you lean to Polish Pans,[95]
You were not born a Pole.
You are a Russian—now confess it—
In Third Division files.[96]

O servant of lords invested with power,
O with what noble daring
You fulminate against free speech
For those whose mouths are stopped![97]

Not to no purpose has your pen
Obeyed[98] aristocrats.
What lackey's school did you attend
To learn this knightly trick?

*҈

Great day of Kiril's death—[99]
What is the simple sincere speech
To honor the sacred remembrance
Of this thousandth anniversary?

What words will stamp this day,
If they be not the words he spoke

[95] Written early in 1869, addressed to the publisher and editor of the journal *Vest'*, Vladimir D. Skaryatin. His attitude was decidedly anti-Slavophile and somewhat aristocratic, contrary to the Slavophile emphasis on the "people." Considering Tyutchev's feelings about the Poles, he could offer Skaryatin no greater insult.

[96] Literally, "only according to the Third Division," who were the Tsarist secret police established by Nicholas I. Tyutchev is accusing Skaryatin of being a police spy.

[97] The last of the Slavophile journals, *Moskva*, was closed down in 1868.

[98] Literally, "served."

[99] Written in early 1869. Sts. Cyril (Kiril) and Methodius, who were brothers, are generally known as the Apostles to the Slavs. It is Cyril who invented the Cyrillic alphabet, adapted from the Greek. He died in 869. His feast day, incidentally, is March 9.

When, bidding farewell to brother and friends,
He left his ashes perforce to Rome.[100]

We, we who share his task
Across whole ages and generations,
We, we have lengthened out his furrow
    Amid seducing lures and doubts.

We too, like him, our work
Unfinished, will leave. Recalling
His sacred words, we then will cry:
"Do not betray yourself, great Russia!

Trust not in aliens, native land,
Their wisdom false, their brazen fraud.
Like holy Kiril, do not forsake
    Your glorious ministry to the Slavs."

TO THE CZECHS
FROM THE MOSCOVITE SLAVS[101] 🔊

On the day of your festival, brothers,
To join with you in rejoicing,
Moscow comes to join you
With reverential hope.

Amid your fervid alarms,
In your great discontent,
She offers you her pledge
Of unity and love.

Accept then from her hand
What long ago was *yours*,
What the old Czech family
Secured at such a price.

So awful was the price
Its memory still remains,[102]

---

[100] A little unfair of Tyutchev, since in Cyril's lifetime the church was after all one.

[101] Written in 1869, on the occasion of the five hundredth anniversary of the birth of Jan Hus and read at a session of the Slavic conference meeting in Moscow. The verses were sent by the conference to Prague along with a golden chalice (see line 17). For the Slavophiles, Hus was a representative of Slavic religiosity revolting against Rome.

[102] That is, the burning of Hus at the stake.

Both your most sanctified
And your most vital source.

Accept the Chalice![103] It sparkled
For you like a star in the night
Of fate and raised your weakness
To superhuman strength.

O now recall how dear
An omen it was for you,
That it was doomed to burn
In eternal flame for you.

The fruits of this great bribe,
Paid by our ancestors
By dint of grievous toil,
Of pain and sacrifice,

You let the insolent lies
Of aliens[104] steal from you,
You let them slander, alas,
God's truth and your fathers' honor.

How long are you condemned
To bear this prison, this prison
Of spirit, most grievous of all,
O consanguineous Czechs?[105]

No, no, your forebears not vainly
Did call Grace down upon you,
And you will understand
The Chalice is your salvation.[106]

HUS AT THE STAKE[107] 🦋

The pyre is built, the fatal flame
Is ready to flare. Silence.

[103] The "chalice" is, of course, the golden present. It is used by Tyutchev as the grail of communion of Orthodoxy and Slavdom as well as a symbol of Hus.

[104] That is, Austria and Roman Catholicism.

[105] Literally, "O Czech people of one blood," i.e., of one blood with the Russians.

[106] Literally, "There is no salvation for you without the chalice."

[107] Written in March 1870, the poem was read at a literary evening at Tyutchev's home on March 26, 1870.

A gentle crackling, and below
The treacherous fire tongues through.

Smoke ran, the nation crowded round;
Now see this tenebrous world:
Oppressors and oppressed, deceit
And force, knighthood and clergy;

Faithbreaking Caesar,[108] the sovereign crowd
Of earthly[109] and spiritual lords,
In sinful infallibility
The Roman hierarch himself;

And she, that naive peasant woman,
In legend still preserved,
Who crossing herself and grieving, brought
Her faggot to the pyre.[110]

And on this pyre, a lamb to slaughter,
That great and just man stands:
He prays, a fiery aureole
About him. His voice is firm.

This holy mentor of the Czech people,
This dauntless witness to Christ
And stern exposer of Roman lies
In lofty modesty.

He never betrayed his God or people,
But fought, invincible,
For God's truth, for its liberty,
For all that Rome named raving.

In spirit in Heaven, in brotherly love
He remains here among his own,
He burned that with his blood he might
Protect Christ's blood for them.

---

[108] The Holy Roman Emperor Sigismund, who assured Hus that he would be safe at the Council of Constance, and then revoked his word as invalid, because it was given to a heretic.

[109] Literally, "imperial lords," that is, lords of the Holy Roman Empire.

[110] According to legend, when an old woman threw some faggots on the fire, Hus called out "Sancta Simplicitas!"

O land of Czechs! O kindred clan!
Preserve your heritage![111]
Complete the spirit's act, the triumph
Of brotherly unity!

Now break the chain with fool-playing Rome[112]
That has so long oppressed you,
And on th' eternal pyre of Hus
Now melt its final link.

TWO UNITIES[113] 🖜

Out of the cup o'erflowing with God's wrath
Blood flows across the land; the West drowns in it.
Blood gushes over you too, our friends and brothers.
    O Slavic world, more tightly close your ranks!

"Our unity," our days' seer[114] has proclaimed,
"Can only be welded together of iron and blood."
But we will try to weld it together of love,
    And we will see which one will last the longer.[115]

[111] Literally, "do not reject your heritage."
[112] This might also be translated "Rome the fool for Christ."
[113] Written in late 1870 and occasioned by the Franco-Prussian War, which had broken out the previous July.
[114] Bismarck.
[115] This second stanza is a summation of the way the Slavophiles saw the difference between the West and Russia.

THE
POLITICAL
LETTERS

RUSSIA AND GERMANY[1] ✍

Dear Editor:

The reception you recently accorded some remarks I took the liberty of addressing to you, as well as the temperate and sensible commentary you made on them, have suggested a fine idea to me. Suppose we try to agree, sir, on the fundamental question? I have not the honor of knowing you personally, so that when I write to you I use the address of the *Augsburg Universal Gazette*. But in the present state of Germany the *Augsburg Gazette* is something more, in my opinion, than a newspaper. It is the first of Germany's political forums. If Germany were fortunate enough to be *one*, there are many ways in which her government could use this newspaper as the legitimate organ of her thought. That is why I address myself to you. I am a Russian, as I have already had the honor of telling you, a Russian in heart and soul, deeply devoted to my country, at peace with my government, and, moreover, totally independent of position. Thus it is a Russian opinion, but a *free* and perfectly *disinterested* one, that I will try to express here.[2]

Be it understood that this letter is addressed more to you than to the public. However, you may make whatever use of it you wish. I am indifferent to publicity. I have no more reason to avoid it than I have to seek it out. Do not fear, sir, that I as a Russian will in my turn plunge into the wretched polemic which a wretched pamphlet has recently stirred up. No, sir, that would hardly be honest.

M. de Custine's book[3] is one more witness of that extravagance of mind, of that intellectual corruption—a typical feature of our time, above all in France—which allows people to treat the most important and loftiest questions more hys-

---

[1] Written while Tyutchev was in Munich in 1844, this article was addressed to Gustav A. Kolb, editor of the Augsburg *Allgemeine Zeitung*. At the time Russia was under attack by many German newspapers as the principal obstacle to German unity. It was also meant as a reply to the attack on Russia by the Marquis de Custine in his *La Russie en 1839*, a book which infuriated many Russian readers. Tyutchev's article was printed both in the *Allgemeine Zeitung* and in brochure form and received the favorable attention of Tsar Nicholas I himself.

[2] At the time Tyutchev had no government position. However, late in 1844 he did re-enter government service, Gregg thinks largely as a result of this article (Gregg, *Fedor Tiutchev*, 15).

[3] *La Russie en 1839* was published in 1843.

terically than reasonably, which permits people to judge a
world with less responsibility than they formerly used for
the analysis of vaudevilles. As for M. de Custine's opponents,
the so-called supporters of Russia, they are certainly more
sincere, but they are quite foolish. They give me the impression of people who through an excess of zeal would precip-
itately open their parasols to protect the peak of Mont Blanc
from the heat of the day. No, sir, an apologia for Russia will
not be the topic of this letter. An apologia for Russia! A
greater master than any of us has undertaken this task, and
it seems to me has so far gloriously acquitted himself. The
real apologist for Russia is History, which for three centuries
has not wearied of having Russia win every trial in which
her mysterious destinies were successively involved. In addressing myself to you, sir, it is of yourself, of your own
country that I wish to speak to you, of its most essential,
most manifest interests; if the question of Russia arises, it
will be only in its direct connections with the destinies of
Germany.

I know that German minds have at no time been so concerned with the great problem of Germanic unity as they are
right now. Well, sir, I will surprise you a great deal, you, an
alert and avant-garde watchman, if I tell you that in the very
midst of this universal concern, the least acute eye would
note tendencies which, if they should grow, would terribly
compromise that end of unity for which all the world seems
to be laboring. One among them is particularly deadly. I will
not say anything that is not in everyone's thought; however,
I could not say one word more without touching on burning
questions; but I am convinced that in our days, as in the
Middle Ages, one with pure hands and honest intentions can
touch anything with impunity.

You are aware, sir, of the nature of the connections which
for thirty years have linked the large and small states of Germany to Russia.[4] I will not here ask you what this or that
opinion, this or that party thinks of these connections; it is
a matter of fact. But the fact is that these connections have
never had more good will, have never been so close, a more
sincerely friendly understanding has never existed between
these different states and Russia. Sir, it is clear to one who

---

[4] That is, since the fall of Napoleon and the creation of the Holy Alliance.

lives in the land of reality and not in the world of preten-
tious talk that this policy is the true, the legitimate policy
of Germany, her proper policy, and that her princes, by
keeping this great tradition of your time of regeneration
unblemished, are only obeying the promptings of the most
enlightened patriotism. But once again, sir, I do not claim
the gift of miracles, I do not claim that I can make everyone share this opinion, above all not those who regard it as
their personal enemy; as well as because this is not at the
moment a matter of opinion, it is a fact, and it seems to me
that the fact is so visible and so tangible that it will encounter
few skeptics.

Need I recount to you, sir, that side by side with and op-
posite to this political course of your governments what
impulse, what inclinations people have ceaselessly worked
for a decade to imprint on German opinion of Russia? Here
again I will refrain, for the moment, from judging at their
true value the complaints, the accusations of all kinds which
are ceaselessly piled up against her with a truly astonishing
perseverance. It is only a matter here of the effect obtained.
It must be admitted that this effect, while not consoling, is
well-nigh total. The laborers have a right to be pleased with
their day's work. This same power which the great generation of 1813 greeted with enthusiastic gratitude, this power
whose faithful alliance, whose active and unselfish friendship has not once in thirty years failed either the peoples
or princes of Germany, they have succeeded, thanks to the
lullabies with which they deluded the childhood of the
present generation, they have almost succeeded, I say, in con-
verting this same power into a bugbear for a great number
of men of our generation, and many energetic minds of our
time have not hesitated to regress to the ingenuous imbecility
of their infancy, pleased to see Russia as the ogre of the
nineteenth century.[5]

All that is true. The enemies of Russia may glory in these
admissions, but let them allow me to continue.

These are the two firmly contrary tendencies; the dissension is glaring and it gets worse every day. On the one side
you have the princes and governments of Germany with
their sober and thoughtful policy, with their fixed course;

---

[5] Much of Western Europe did indeed see Russia in this light at the time.

and on the other side another prince of the time—opinion, which drifts wherever wind and wave may push it.[6]

Sir, allow me to appeal to your patriotism and to your intelligence: what do you think of this state of affairs? What results do you expect for the interests, for the future of your country? For, understand me rightly, it is a matter of Germany alone at the moment. My God, if but one among you suspected how little Russia is affected by all this violent activity directed against her, it might make her most rancorous enemies think twice.

It is obvious that so long as peace endures this dissension will not lead to any serious and overt disturbance; the evil will run on underground; your governments, as is reasonable, will not change their direction, will not turn the whole foreign policy of Germany upside down in order to adapt themselves to some fanatic or muddleheaded minds; the latter, urged, impelled by opposition, will not believe they can be overcommitted to the direction most contrary to the one they reject; and thus it is that, even while continuing to speak of the unity of Germany, they will come closer, eyes constantly turned towards Germany, they will come closer to a fatal fall backwards, so to speak, a fall into the abyss into which your country has more than once slipped. I am quite well aware, sir, that so long as we keep the peace the danger I point out will be only imaginary; but once the crisis comes, that crisis a foreboding of which weighs upon Europe,[7] once the days of storm come, a storm which will come to a head in no time at all, which will push all tendencies to their furthest limits, which will tear the final word from all opinions, from all parties—what, sir, will happen then? Would it therefore follow that there is for nations, even more than for individuals, an inexorable, inexpiable fate? Must we believe there are tendencies in them stronger than all their will, than all their reason, organic maladies which no skill, no regimen, can cope with? Would it be so with that terrible tendency to intestine discord which we see reborn in all the great epochs of your noble country's history like an ill-omened phoenix? This tendency, which exploded in the Middle Ages in the blasphemous and anti-Christian duel between Papacy and Empire, which caused the parricidal

---

[6] This is typical of Tyutchev's antidemocratic approach.
[7] That is, increasing revolutionary activity in Western Europe.

struggle between the Emperor and the barons, then, after a
momentary weakness brought on by Germany's exhaustion,
acquired new strength and was renovated in the Reformation,
and, after having accepted a final form and a kind of legal
conspiracy from it, set to work more zealously than ever,
embracing all flags, espousing all causes, always the same
under different names until the moment when, having reached
the decisive crisis of the Thirty Years' War, it called the
foreigner to its aid, first Sweden, and then finally entered
into partnership with the enemy, with France, and thanks to
this grouping of forces, in less than two centuries gloriously concluded the commission of death with which it was
charged.[8]

These are baleful memories! How is it that with memories
like these you do not feel more alarmed by all the signs which
augur a budding antagonism in your country's frame of
mind? How is it that you do not ask yourself in terror if this
is not the re-awakening of your ancient and terrible disease?

The past thirty years can undoubtedly be numbered among
the finest of your history; finer days have not shone on
Germany since the great reigns of its Salic emperors; not
for many centuries has Germany been so completely master
of herself, felt herself so much *one*, so much herself; not for
many centuries has she had a stronger, a more imposing
posture in regard to her eternal rival. She has kept that rival
in check everywhere. See for yourself: your most glorious
emperors have never wielded a more real authority beyond
the Alps than German power wields now.[9] The Rhine has
become German again, heart and soul; Belgium, which the
last European commotion seemed about to throw into the
arms of France, stopped on the brink, and it is now obvious
that she is going back to you; the region of Burgundy is
taking shape again; Holland sooner or later will be unable
to avoid coming back to you.[10] Such, then, is the final result
of the great struggle in which France and you have been
involved for more than two centuries; your triumph is complete, you have had the last word. Nevertheless, admit it:
for anyone who had watched this struggle from its begin-

[8] It was precisely a Franco-German rapprochement which worried Russia
most at the time.
[9] That is, in northern Italy, then a part of Austria-Hungary.
[10] Tyutchev was being a little over-optimistic—obviously.

ning, for anyone who had followed it through all its stages,
through all its fortunes up to the eve of the crowning and
decisive day, it would have been hard to foresee a like conclusion; appearances were not for you, the odds were not
in your favor. Since the end of the Middle Ages, despite a
few checks,[11] France's power had not stopped growing,
centralizing and controlling itself, and it is at the end of this
era that the Empire, thanks to the religious split, entered
upon its last period, the period of its legal dissolution; even
the victories you gained were barren for you, for these victories did not stop the inner dissolution; indeed, they often
only made it go faster. Under Louis XIV, even though the
great king came to grief, France triumphed, her influence
ruled supreme over Germany; finally came the Revolution,
which, after having expunged from the French nationality
the last traces of its extraction, of its Germanic relationships,[12]
after having given France its solely Roman disposition, began
against Germany, against the very principle of its existence,
a last struggle, a struggle to the death; and it is at the moment
that the soldier crowned by this Revolution[13] had his parody
of the Empire of Charlemagne produced on the very remains
of the Empire founded by Charlemagne, forcing the peoples
of Germany, as their final humiliation, to play their part in
it too, it is at this crowning moment that the upset occurred
and everything was transformed.

How was it created, that stupendous upset? By whom?
What had brought it about? It was brought about by the
advent of a third power on the field of battle of the European
West; but this third power was a whole world.

Here, sir, you must allow me a short digression, so that we
may understand each other. People talk a lot about Russia; in
our days she is the object of an eager, of an anxious curiosity.
It is clear that she has become one of the great concerns of the
century; but, in contrast with the other problems that excite
it, this one, it must be admitted, depresses rather than stimu-
lates contemporary thought. And it could not be otherwise: contemporary thought, daughter of the West, feels
it is facing a factor if not hostile, at least definitely foreign, a
factor that challenges it, and one would say that it is afraid of

[11] The sixteenth century and the Wars of Religion in particular.
[12] That is, France was settled by Germanic tribes.
[13] That is, Napoleon.

losing its position, of calling its own legitimacy into question
if it should accept as entirely legitimate the question put to
it, if it should apply itself earnestly and conscientiously to
understanding and solving that question. What is Russia?
What is her justification, her historical law? Whence does
she come? Where is she going? What does she represent?
It is true that the world has made a place for her in the sun;
but the philosophy of history has still not deigned to assign
her one. A few exceptional intellects—two or three in Germany, one or two in France, freer, more advanced than the
majority—have indeed caught a glimpse of the problem,
have, indeed, raised a corner of the veil, but up to now their
words have been little understood, or little heeded.

For a long time the way in which Russia has been understood in the West has in some respects resembled the first
impressions of Columbus' contemporaries. It was the same
mistake, the same optical illusion. You know that for a long
time men of the old continent, while applauding the immortal discovery, still stubbornly refused to acknowledge
the existence of a new continent; they found it easier and
more rational to assume that the lands which had just been
revealed to them were only an extension, a prolongation
of the continent they already knew. The same kind of ideas
has long been held of this other new world, Eastern Europe,
of which Russia has always been the soul, the driving force,
and on which she was called to impose her glorious name,
as the price of the historical existence which this world has
already received from her, or awaits from her. For centuries
the European West believed in all good faith that there was
not, that there could not be any other Europe than itself. It
knew, as a matter of fact, that there were peoples and realms
beyond its borders which called themselves Christian; in
times of strength it had even penetrated the edges of this
nameless world, it had torn away some scraps of it which
it incorporated into itself after a fashion, by perverting them,
by de-nationalizing them;[14] but that beyond this furthest
border there was another Europe, an Eastern Europe, a quite
legitimate sister of the Christian West, Christian like it, not
feudal, not hierarchic, it is true, but by the same token more

---

[14] Tyutchev is thinking in particular of the Slavs in the Austro-Hungarian
Empire.

deeply Christian; that there was a whole world there, one
in its principles, interdependent in its parts, living its own
organic, special life: that is what it was impossible to acknowledge, that is what many people, even in our days,
would like to call in doubt. For a long time the mistake had
been excusable; for centuries the driving force had remained
as though buried in chaos: its movement had been slow and
almost imperceptible; a thick cloud shrouded this slow fashioning of a world. But finally, when the time was ripe, a
giant's hand destroyed the cloud and the Europe of Charlemagne found itself face to face with the Europe of Peter the
Great.

Once this is recognized, everything becomes clear, everything is explained: now we understand the real reason for
Russia's rapid progress, for its stupendous growth, which
has astonished the world. We understand that the alleged
conquests, the alleged violent activity have been the most
organic and the most legitimate work history has ever carried
out, it was plainly an enormous restoration that was being
performed. We will also understand why we have seen all
irregular tendencies, influences, and institutions faithless
to the great principle she represented that Russia met on
her road successively perish and be obliterated under her
hand, why Poland had to perish, not the singularity of the
Polish race, God forbid, but the false civilization, the false
nationality that had been ascribed to it.[15] It is also from this
point of view that we will better appreciate the real significance of what is called the Eastern question,[16] that question
which we pretend to declare insoluble, precisely because for
a long time everyone has anticipated the inevitable solution.
Indeed, it is a matter of knowing if Eastern Europe, already
three-quarters formed, if this real empire of the East, of
which the first, that of the Byzantine Caesars, of the ancient
Orthodox Emperors, had been only a weak and unfinished
sketch, whether or not Eastern Europe will receive its last,
its most essential complement;[17] if it will procure it in the
normal course of events or will be forced to try its fortune
at arms, at the risk of great disasters for the world. But let us
return to our subject.

[15] By Roman Catholicism, in particular.
[16] That is, the question of Russia's place in Europe.
[17] That is, Constantinople.

That, sir, was the third power whose arrival on the scene of action abruptly settled the age-long struggle of the European West; only the appearance of Russia in your ranks has brought unity, and unity has given you victory.

And now, in order to give ourselves a true account of the way things stand at present, we cannot be too much aware of one truth, which is that since the intervention of the organized East in the affairs of the West, everything is changed in Europe: until then you were two, now we are three. Prolonged struggles have become impossible.

The three following arrangements, the only ones possible henceforth, can result from the current state of affairs. Germany will keep her preponderance in the center of Europe as a staunch ally of Russia; otherwise this preponderance will pass into the hands of France. But do you know, sir, what the preponderance in France's hands would mean for you? It would mean, if not sudden death, at least the sure decline of Germany. There remains the third arrangement, the one that would perhaps please some people most: Germany allied with France against Russia. Alas, sir, this arrangement has already been tried, in 1812, and, as you know, it had very little success. Besides, I do not think that after the conclusion of the thirty years which have just elapsed Germany was in any mood to accept just a place in a new confederation of the Rhine: for every close alliance with France can never be other than that for Germany. Do you know, sir, what Russia meant to do when she intervened in this struggle between the two principles, between the two great nationalities which have for centuries disputed the European West, and decided the struggle in favor of Germany, of the Germanic principle? She wanted once and for all to carry the day for the right, for historical legitimacy, over the revolutionary process. And why did she want to do that? Because the right, historical legitimacy, is her cause, her own cause, the cause of her future, it is the right that she demands for herself and for her own. Only the blindest ignorance willfully closing its eyes to the light could still disregard this great truth, for in the long run is it not in the name of this right, of this historical legitimacy, that Russia raised a whole race, a whole world, from its disgrace, that she summoned it to live its own life, that she restored its autonomy to it, that she re-created it? And it is also in the name of this same right that she will be able to stop political experimenters from tearing or tricking whole

populations from their center of living unity, in order later
to carve them up more easily and mold them like dead
things, at the pleasure of their innumerable caprices, in short,
so that they may not detach the living limbs from the body
to which they belong, on the pretext that this will assure
them greater freedom of movement.

The immortal honor of the sovereign who is now on the
throne of Russia[18] is that he is making himself more completely, more energetically than any of his predecessors the
intelligent and unbending representative of this right, of this
historical legitimacy. Once Russia's choice was made, Europe
knows whether she remained faithful to it for thirty years.
We can assert, history book in hand, that it would be extremely difficult to find in the political annals of the world a
second example of an alliance as profoundly moral as the
one which for thirty years has linked the princes of Germany
to Russia, and it is this great character of morality which has
made it last, which has helped it to resolve many difficulties,
to overcome many obstacles, and now, after the test of good
and evil days, this alliance has overcome its last test, the most
significant of all: the inspiration on which it was based has
been transmitted, without shock and without change, from
the first founders to their heirs.

Well, sir, ask your governments if Russia's solicitude for
the great political interests of Germany has belied itself even
once during the past thirty years. Ask men who have been
involved if this solicitude has not many times and on many
questions outstripped your own patriotic promptings. For
some years you in Germany have been deeply concerned
with the question of Germanic unity. It has not always been
so, you know. I who have lived a long time among you, I
could, if need be, recall the precise period when this question
began to excite people; certainly there was little question of
this unity, at least in the press, at the period when every
liberal sheet thought it a matter of conscience to grab every
chance to address the same insults to Austria and her government that are now lavished on Russia. To be sure, the concern is most praiseworthy, unquestionably very legitimate,
but it is of rather recent date. It is true that Russia has never
preached the unity of Germany, but for thirty years she has
not ceased, on every occasion and in every way, to recom-

[18] Nicholas I.

mend to Germany union, harmony, mutual confidence, voluntary subordination of individual interests to the great cause of the general interest, and she has never wearied of constantly reproducing these counsels, these exhortations, of multiplying them, with all the energetic freedom of a perfectly disinterested zeal.

Some years ago a book much talked about in Germany and to which an official source was quite falsely imputed, seemed to give standing among you to the opinion that at a certain period Russia's policy was especially to attach second-rank German states to itself to the detriment of the legitimate influence of the two great states of the Confederation.[19] No assumption has been more gratuitous and even, I must say, more completely contrary to reality. Consult competent men on the subject, they will tell you what it is all about; perhaps they will tell you that in its constant concern to assure the political independence of Germany above all, Russian diplomacy sometimes laid itself open to bruising pardonably sensitive persons by too insistently recommending to the small courts of Germany that they stick to the system of the two great powers in all circumstances. Perhaps this is the place to judge at its true value another accusation a thousand times brought forth against Russia and no truer than the first. What has not been said to spread the belief that it is her influence above all which has blocked the development of constitutional government in Germany? Generally speaking, it is superlatively irrational to try to turn Russia into a systematic adversary of this or that form of government; how, great God, could she have become what she is, how could she exercise on the world the influence she does with a like narrowness of ideas? Furthermore, in the particular case under review, it is strictly true to say that Russia has always energetically declared for the loyal support of established institutions, for religious reverence for contracts entered into; in pursuit of that aim it is quite possible that she thought that it would not be prudent, would not be in the most vital interest of Germany (her unity) to give parliamentary privilege in the constitutional states of the Confederation the same range that it has, for example, in England or France; that if even at the moment it was not always easy to establish that agreement, that perfect under-

[19] Prussia and Austria.

standing among the states that joint action entails, the problem would become simply insoluble in a Germany dominated, that is to say, divided, by a half dozen sovereign houses
of Parliament. That is one of the truths now accepted by all
well-disposed people in Germany. Russia's only fault was to
understand this about ten years too soon.

Passing now from these internal questions to the external
situation, I will speak to you, sir, of the July Revolution and
of the results it probably should have had for your country
and did not have. Need I tell you that the principle of this
explosion, that the very soul of this movement was above all
the need for violent revenge on Europe, and principally on
you, it was the irresistible need to regain that preponderance
in the West which France had so long enjoyed and which
it resentfully saw in your hands for thirty years? I certainly
give full credit to the king of the French,[20] I admire his
ability, I wish long life to him and to his system. But what
would have happened, sir, if every time since 1835 the French
government tried to cast its eyes over the horizon of Germany it had not constantly met on the throne of Russia the
same firm and decided attitude, the same caution, the same
coolness, and above all the same faithfulness, in all circumstances, to established alliances, to contracts entered into?
If he had been able to surprise just one moment of doubt,
of wavering, don't you think that the Napoleon of peace
himself would finally have wearied of always holding back
this France trembling under his hand and would have let it
go? And what would have happened if he had been able to
count on complicity?

Sir, I was in Germany when M. Thiers,[21] giving in to a
so-to-speak instinctive impulse, was getting ready to do what
seemed to him the simplest and most natural thing in the
world, that is, to take revenge on Germany for the checks
to his diplomacy in the East; I was a witness of the explosion,
of the truly national wrath that this ingenuous impudence
provoked among you, and I am happy to have seen it; since

---

[20] Louis-Philippe.

[21] Adolphe Thiers (1797–1877), prime minister of France in 1836 and
1840, and president of France in 1871, was a strong supporter of revolutionary
and Napoleonic ideals. Guided always by an intense love of country, he
believed strongly that political power should be in the hands of the middle
class.

then I have always heard the *Rheinlied* sung with much
pleasure. But, sir, how is it that your political press, which
knows everything, which knows, for example, the exact
number of pistol shots exchanged on the Prussian frontier
between Russian customs officers and Prussian smugglers,
how is it, I say, that it did not know what went on at that
time between the courts of Germany and Russia? How is it
that it did not know, or did not inform you, that at the first
sign of enmity from France 80,000 Russian troops would
have marched to the aid of your threatened independence,
and that 200,000 men would have followed them in six
weeks? Well, sir, this circumstance did not remain unknown
in Paris, and perhaps you will think, as I do, whatever value
I put on the *Rheinlied*, that it contributed not a little to the
old *Marseillaise*'s decision to beat such a prompt retreat
before her young rival.

I mentioned the press. Do not think, sir, that I have any
hidebound prejudices against the German press, or that I am
bitter at its unspeakable ill will towards us. Not at all, I
assure you; I am quite ready to do it honor for the good
qualities it has, and I would like to attribute a part at least of
its faults and errors of taste to the uncommon government
under which it lives. Certainly there is no lack of talent, of
ideas, nor even of patriotism in your periodical press; in
many ways it is the legitimate daughter of your noble and
great literature, that literature which has restored a feeling of
national identity among you. What is missing in your press,
and that to a dangerous degree, is political sensitivity, a lively
and secure understanding of the facts of the situation, of the
real environment in which it lives. Also noteworthy, in its
revelations as in its tendencies, is something improvident,
something ill-considered, in short, a moral irresponsibility
which perhaps proceeds from that state of prolonged ado-
lescence in which it still is.

How else can it be explained, in fact, if not by this consciousness of its moral irresponsibility, this intense, blind,
frantic hostility to Russia in which it has indulged for many
years? Why? To what end? To whose benefit? Does it seem
even once to have earnestly examined, from the point of
view of Germany's political interest, the possible, the probable results of what it was doing? Has it even once earnestly
wondered if it has not, by laboring with incredible tenacity
to embitter, to poison, irretrievably to jeopardize the

reciprocal arrangements between the countries, if it has not
been fashioning the destruction of the very basis of the system
of alliances on which the power of Germany relative to
Europe rests? If it is not trying with every means in its power
to substitute for the most favorable political arrangement that
history has ever effected for your country the most positively
disastrous arrangement? Does not this irrepressible impro-
vidence remind you, sir, of the child's prank of your great
Goethe which he so gracefully recounts in his memoirs? You
remember the time when the little Wolfgang, left alone in
the house, could think of no better way of spending his time
during the absence of his parents than that of successively
throwing out of the window all his mother's kitchen utensils
he could get his hands on, enjoying and being delighted with
the noise they made when they fell and broke on the pave-
ment. It is true that across the way was a wicked neighbor
whose encouragement provoked the child to keep up his
clever game; but you, sir, you have not even the excuse of a
similar provocation.

If even one could discover a sensible cause for all this
torrent of spiteful ranting against Russia, an agreed-upon
cause to justify so much hate! I know that if need be I could
find lunatics who would tell me as gravely as can be: "We
must hate you; your principle, the very principle of your
civilization, is antipathetic to us Germans, to us Westerners;
you have had neither *Feudalism* nor *Pontifical Hierarchy*; you
have experienced neither the wars of *Church* and *Empire* nor
the wars of *Religion*, or even the *Inquisition*; you have not
taken part in the Crusades, you have not known Chivalry,
four centuries ago you achieved a unity we are still looking
for, your principle does not assign a large enough role to
individual liberty, it does not sufficiently authorize division,
breaking up."[22] All that is true; but be just—has all that
hindered us from bravely and loyally helping you when it
was a question of your asserting, of your regaining your
political independence, your nationality, and now is not the
least you can do to allow us ours? Let us speak in earnest,

---

[22] For those of Tyutchev's persuasion, this was a spiritual as well as a
political statement. It was the oneness and wholeness of Russia that was
important, in contrast with the divisiveness, the anarchy, indeed, of the
West. Cf. Dostoevsky, *The Diary of a Writer*, and Gogol, *Selected Passages
from Correspondence with Friends*.

this matter deserves it. Russia asks no more than to respect your historical legitimacy, the historical legitimacy of the peoples of the West; for at least thirty years she has dedicated herself, with you, to lifting it up again, to putting it back on its foundation; she is thus quite prepared to respect it not only in principle, but even in its most extreme consequences, even in its deviations, even in its failings; but you too, you in your turn must learn to respect us in our unity and our strength.

Will I be told that it is the flaws in our social structure, the defects of our administration, the state of our lower classes, etc., etc., that these are the things that excite opinion against Russia? Really! Could this be true? I who a moment ago thought I was complaining of an excess of ill will, will I now be obliged to protest against an overdone sympathy? After all, we are not alone in the world, and if you have in fact such a superfluous depth of human sympathy and you have no room for it at home and for your own, would it not be just for you at least to distribute it in a more equitable fashion among the various peoples of this earth? Everyone, alas, needs pity. Look at England, for example; what do you say of it? Look at its manufacturing population. Look at Ireland. If you could with perfect knowledge determine the respective balance sheets of the two countries, if you had a fair scale to weigh the miseries brought in their train by Russian barbarism and English civilization, perhaps you would find more point than exaggeration in the statement of the man who, equally a foreigner in both countries, but one who knew them both profoundly, affirmed with complete conviction that "there are at least a million men in the United Kingdom who would be much better off if they were sent to Siberia."

Ah, sir, what keeps you Germans, who in so many ways have an indisputable moral superiority over your neighbors across the Rhine, what keeps you from borrowing a little of their good common sense, of their lively intelligence so certain of their own interests which characterizes them? They too have a press, newspapers which revile us, which vie with one another in tearing us apart, without respite, without measure, without shame. Look, for example, at the Parisian press, that hundred-eyed hydra jetting fire and flame against us. What rages! What explosions! What uproar! Well, but let Paris be assured this very day that the reconciliation so ardently desired is about to be accomplished, that the advances so often made have finally been welcomed, and tomorrow you will see all this hate-filled din die down, all this brilliant pyrotechnic of insults vanish, and from these extinct volcanoes, from these pacified mouths will issue diversely warbling voices—but all equally melodious—with the last wreath of smoke, all vying to celebrate our happy reconciliation.

But this letter is too long, it is time to close. Allow me, sir, in conclusion, to summarize my thoughts in a few words.

I addressed myself to you with no other aim than the one I maintain by virtue of my free and personal conviction. I am under no one's orders, I am no one's mouthpiece; my thought is independent. But I certainly have every reason to believe that if the contents of this letter were known in Russia, public opinion would not hesitate to endorse them. Up to now Russian opinion has only been indifferently affected by all the hue and cry of the German press, not that the opinions, not that the sensibilities of Germany were indifferent to it, certainly not. But she was loath to take seriously all these violent words, all these shots in the air in honor of Russia; in all of it she saw at most an entertainment in bad taste. Russian opinion definitely refuses to grant that a sober, serious, loyal, deeply fair nation, such as the world has known Germany to be through all the periods of its history, that this nation, I say, would slough off its nature to disclose another made in the image of some temperamental or muddleheaded beings, of some ranters either over-excited or of bad faith; that, denying the past, misconstruing the present, and imperiling the future, Germany would agree to welcome, to nurture a wicked sentiment, a sentiment unworthy of it, simply to have the pleasure of making a great political blunder. No, it is not possible!

I addressed myself to you, sir, because I recognize that the *Universal Gazette* is more than a newspaper for Germany; it is a force, a force which, I gladly proclaim, to a high degree unites national sensibility with political intelligence: it is in the name of this two-fold authority that I have tried to speak of you.

The frame of mind which people have created, which people are trying to propagate in Germany in regard to Russia is not yet dangerous, but it bids fair to become so. This frame of mind will change nothing, I am convinced, so far as the current relations between the German and Russian governments are concerned; but it is tending more and more to warp public conscience on one of the most important questions there is for a nation, the question of its alliances. By presenting the most national policy that Germany has ever followed in the falsest colors, it tends to set mind against mind, to push the most vehement, the most thoughtless ones into ways full of danger, into ways where Germany's fortune has already more than once gone astray. Should a crisis erupt in Europe, should the age-long quarrel, decided thirty years ago in your favor, flare up again, your princes certainly will not find Russia wanting, any more than Russia will find them wanting; but it is also then that we would probably have to reap what is being sown today: the division of persons will have borne its fruits, and these fruits will be bitter for Germany; I fear there would be new desertions and new factions. And then, sir, you would have too cruelly expiated the wrong of once having been unjust to us.

That, sir, is what I had to say to you. You may make whatever use of my words you see fit.

RUSSIA AND THE REVOLUTION[23] 🌿

In order to understand what the supreme crisis upon which Europe has just entered is all about, the following must be realized. For a long time there have been only two real powers in Europe, "the Revolution and Russia." These two powers are now facing each other, and tomorrow perhaps they will be grappling with each other. There is no possible treaty or compromise between them. The life of one is the death of the other. On the result of the struggle between them, the greatest struggle the world has witnessed, depends the entire political and religious future of humanity for centuries.

The fact of this antagonism is now obvious to everyone, but such is the lack of intelligence of a century stupified by argumentation that, even while living face to face with this huge fact, the current generation is far from having grasped its true character and appreciated its causes.

Up to now people have sought the explanation in a sphere of purely political ideas; it is by the differences of a purely human order of principles that they have tried to account for it. No, certainly, the dispute which divides the Revolution and Russia has far more profound causes; it can be summarized in a few words.

Russia is above all a Christian Empire; the Russian people is Christian not only by the Orthodoxy of its beliefs, but by something more deep-seated even than belief. It is so by that faculty of renunciation and sacrifice which forms the basis of its moral nature. The Revolution is, first and foremost, anti-Christian. The anti-Christian spirit is the soul of the Revolution; that is its specific, essential character; the forms it has successively assumed, the slogans it has by turns adopted, everything including its violent acts and crimes, have only been accessory or accidental; but what is not so is the anti-Christian principle that animates it, and it is to this also, it must be said, that it owes its terrible power over the world. Whoever does not understand that has for sixty years[24] been blind to the spectacle the world offers him.

The human ego which wants to depend only on itself, which neither recognizes nor accepts any other law than that

---

[23] Written in April 1848 and originally intended to be a chapter in a larger, never-completed work, *Russia and the West*, this article was printed separately in Paris in 1849.

[24] That is, since the French Revolution of 1789.

of its own pleasure, the human ego, in short, which substitutes
itself for God is certainly not something new among men;
but what is new is this absolutism of the human ego exalted
into a political and social right and with this claim aspiring
to take over society. It is that new invention which in 1789
was called the French Revolution.

Since then, and through all its metamorphoses, the Revolution has remained true to its nature, and at perhaps no other
moment of its tenure has it felt more itself, more deeply
anti-Christian than at the present moment when it has just
adopted the slogan of Christianity, brotherhood. It is indeed that which might lead one to think it has reached its
apogee. In fact, after listening to all those ingenuously blasphemous declamations that have become a kind of official
language of the time, who would not believe that the new
French Republic has come to the world solely in order to
fulfill the law of the Gospel? It is also to this very mission
that the warrants it has created are solemnly attributed,
always excepting an amendment that the Revolution keeps
in reserve: for the spirit of humility and self-renunciation,
the whole basis of Christianity, it means to substitute the
spirit of pride and dominance; for free and voluntary charity
an obligatory charity; and in place of the brotherhood
preached and accepted in the name of God, it claims to establish a brotherhood imposed through fear of the sovereign
mass. These differences aside, its reign in fact promises to be
that of Christ.

And let no one be led into error by that species of con-
temptuous good will which the new authorities have thus
far shown to the Catholic Church and its ministers. This
perhaps is the most serious indication of the state of affairs
and the most certain mark of the omnipotence the Revolution
has acquired. Why, in fact, should the Revolution be stern
with a clergy, with Christian priests who not only submit to
it, accept it and adopt it, who in order to exorcise it glorify
all its violence, and who, without believing in it, share in
all its lies? If there were only calculation in conduct like this,
the calculation would already be apostasy; but if conviction
comes into it, it is something a good deal more.

Nevertheless, we foresee that there will be no lack of per-
secutions; for the day that the limit of concessions is reached,
the day that the Catholic Church believes it must resist, we
will see that it can do so only by retreating to martyrdom.

The Revolution can be trusted: in all things it will prove faithful to itself and consistent to the end.

The explosion of February has done this great service to the world; it has made the whole structure of illusions with which reality had been masked collapse to the ground. The least intelligent people should by now understand that the history of Europe for thirty years has been only one long swindle. Indeed, with what pitiless light is not all this past, so close and already so far from us, suddenly illuminated? Who, for example, does not now understand what ludicrous pretention there was in that wisdom of the century which was sanctimoniously satisfied that it had succeeded in subduing the Revolution by the exorcism of a constitution, in binding its terrible energy by a legal formula? Who can still doubt, after what has happened, that from the moment the revolutionary principle has entered the blood of a society all its processes, all its formulae for transactions are no more than drugs which can put a sick man to sleep temporarily, but do not stop the sickness from going its way?

That is why, after having devoured the Restoration, which, as the last remains of legitimate authority in France, was personally loathsome to it, the Revolution has no better suffered that other power, born of itself, which it willingly accepted in 1830 as an accomplice against Europe, but which it broke the day that this power presumed to think itself the Revolution's master instead of its servant.

Allow me a reflection at this time. How is it that among all the princes of Europe, as well as among the politicians who have controlled it in recent times, there has been only one who immediately recognized and pointed out the great illusion of 1830, and who since, alone in Europe, alone perhaps among his advisors, has steadfastly refused to allow himself to be overcome by it? It is because at this time there was fortunately on the throne of Russia a sovereign in whom Russian thought was embodied, and because in the current state of the world Russian thought is the only one sufficiently outside the revolutionary environment to be able clearly to appraise the events taking place.

What the Emperor foresaw in 1830 the Revolution has not failed to carry into effect, point by point. All the concessions, all the sacrifices of principle made by monarchic Europe to the creation of July in the interest of a shadow of the *status quo*, all this the Revolution seized so that it might turn it to use for the upheaval it had in mind, and while the legitimate authorities were following a more or less skillful diplomacy with the quasi-legitimacy and the statesmen and diplomats of all Europe were attending the parliamentary jousts of Paris as interested and benevolent patrons, the revolutionary party was almost openly working without respite to mine the ground under their feet.

It could be said that the great task of the party for these last eighteen years has been to revolutionize Germany from top to bottom, and we can now judge whether this task has been well discharged.

Germany is assuredly the country about which people have had the strangest illusions for the longest time. It was thought to be an orderly country, because it was tranquil and because nobody wanted to see the appalling anarchy that had overrun it and played havoc with its men of intellect.

Sixty years of a destructive philosophy have completely disintegrated all Christian beliefs and in this denial of all faith have developed the prime revolutionary sentiment: intellectual pride, so that at the present time there is perhaps no place where this plague of the century goes deeper and is more poisonous than in Germany. By a necessary consequence, Germany feels its hatred for Russia grow in proportion to the extent to which it is revolutionized. In fact, because of the kindnesses Germany received from her, a revolutionary Germany could have only an implacable hatred for Russia. At the present moment this paroxysm of hatred seems to have reached its height; because in Germany it has overcome —I do not say this lightly— the very instinct of self-preservation itself.[25]

If such a melancholy hatred could inspire anything but pity, Russia certainly would be sufficiently revenged by the spectacle Germany gave to the world after the February Revolution. For perhaps never before in history have we seen a whole people plagiarizing another at the very moment when the other is giving itself up to the most unbridled violence.

And let it not be said, to justify all these so obviously artificial movements which have just overturned the whole

[25] See above, "Russia and Germany."

political order of Germany and are putting the very existence
of the social order itself in jeopardy, that they have been
inspired by a broadly experienced, sincere feeling, the need
for Germany unity. This feeling is sincere, agreed; this wish
is that of the great majority, I have no objection; but what
does that prove? It is one of the maddest illusions of our
time to fancy that it is enough for something to be eagerly,
ardently desired by the great mass for it to become, for that
reason alone, inevitably realizable. Besides, it must be recognized that in the society of our time there is no wish, no
need (however sincere, however legitimate it be) that the
Revolution, by making it its own, does not pervert and turn
into a lie, and it is exactly this that has happened with the
question of German unity: for from now on it must be clear
to anyone who has not given up all ability to acknowledge
the evidence that the path Germany has just taken in its search
for a solution to the problem will end not in unity, but in a
frightful tearing asunder, in some supreme and irreparable
disaster.

Yes, certainly, we can no longer defer recognizing that the
only unity possible, not for Germany as the newspapers make
it, but for the real Germany as history has made it, the only
chance for a serious and practical unity for this country was
indissolubly bound to the political system it has just broken.

If for these last thirty-three years,[26] perhaps the happiest
of all its history, Germany has fashioned a body politic hier-
archically composed and operating on orderly lines, on what
terms could such a result have been obtained and ensured?
It was obviously on the terms of a sincere agreement between
the two principles which have been fighting over this country
for more than three centuries. But does anyone believe that
this agreement itself, so slow to be established, so difficult to
maintain, would have been possible, that it could have lasted
so long if Austria and Prussia were not, after the great wars
against France, closely allied to Russia, firmly supported by
her? That is the political arrangement which, by realizing for
Germany the only system of unity applicable to it, was worth
to it this thirty-three-year truce which it has just broken.

There is no hatred, no lie which can ever prevail against
this fact. In a fit of madness Germany has indeed been able
to break an alliance which, without imposing any sacrifice

[26] That is, since 1815 and the establishment of the Holy Alliance.

on it, ensured and protected its national independence, but by doing so Germany has forever deprived herself of any firm and lasting foundation.

You can see the demonstration of this truth in the second proof, events, in this terrible time when events move almost as fast as the human word. It is hardly two months since the Revolution in Germany has been at work, and already, to be just to it, the work of destruction in this country is further advanced than it was by Napoleon after ten of his crushing campaigns.

Look at Austria, more imperiled, more battered, more disabled than in 1809. Look at Prussia, doomed to suicide by its fatal and forced complicity with the Polish party. Look at the lands of the Rhine where, in spite of songs and phrases, the Rhenish Confederation aims only at rebirth. Anarchy everywhere, authority nowhere, and all under the attack of a France where a social revolution asks only to boil over into the political revolution which is at work in Germany.

From now on, for every sensible man the question of German unity is a settled question. One would have to have the kind of fatuousness proper to German ideologues seriously to wonder if the gang of journalists, lawyers, and professors now meeting in Frankfort[27] who are taking on the mission of reviving Charlemagne have any appreciable chance of succeeding in the work they have undertaken, if their hands will be powerful and dexterous enough to re-raise the inverted pyramid by balancing it on its point in this trembling soil.

That is no longer the question; it is no longer a matter of knowing whether Germany will be one, but whether out of these inner discords probably complicated by a foreign war it will succeed in salvaging any shred of its national existence.

The parties which are going to tear this country apart are already beginning to take form. The Republic has already taken hold at different points in Germany, and we can count on its not withdrawing without a fight against it, for it has logic for it and France behind it. In the eyes of this party there is neither sense nor value to the question of nationality. It will not hesitate one instant in the interest of its cause to sacrifice the independence of its country, and it would enlist

[27] The delegates to Frankfort were supposed to set up a German Union, but they bogged down in internecine quarrels.

all Germany as soon as possible under the flag of France, even if it be under the red flag. Its collaborators are everywhere; it finds aid and support in men as in things, as much in the anarchic instincts of the masses as in the anarchic institutions which have just been so profusely seeded throughout Germany. But its best, its most powerful collaborators are precisely those men who at any moment might be called to fight against it; so much are these men bound to it by solidarity of principles. Now the whole question is one of knowing if the struggle will break out before the divisions and follies of the alleged conservatives have had the time to jeopardize all the elements of strength and resistance of which Germany still disposes; whether, in short, when they are attacked by the republican party they make up their minds to see it as in fact it is, the advance guard of the French invasion, and whether the feeling of the peril with which national independence would be threatened restores enough energy to them to battle against the republic to the death; or, in order to escape the struggle, they would rather accept some pretense of a settlement, which for them would really be only a disguised surrender. In the case that the second conjecture becomes fact, then, it must be admitted, the possibility of a crusade against Russia, of that crusade which has always been the cherished dream of the Revolution and which has now become its war-cry—that possibility would be transformed almost into a certainty; the day of the crucial struggle would be at hand, and it is Poland which would be the battlefield.[28] That at any rate is the fortune which the revolutionaries of all countries lovingly hope for; but there is an ingredient in the question they have not taken sufficiently into account, and this omission could singularly upset their calculations.

The revolutionary party, in Germany above all, appears to be convinced that, since it sells the national ingredient so cheaply itself, it would be the same in all countries subjected to it and that everywhere and always the question of principle would take precedence over the question of nationality. Events in Lombardy should already have given pause to the student reformers of Vienna, who fancied it was enough to

[28] The question of the freedom of Poland was much debated by the revolutionary parties in Western Europe, particularly by the German ones (after all, Prussia and Austria had participated in the dismemberment of Poland), but no more than expressions of sympathy were sent to Poland.

kick out Prince Metternich and proclaim freedom of the
press to resolve the fearful difficulties weighing upon the
Austrian monarchy. The Italians have no less persisted in
seeing in them only *Tedeschi* and *Barbari*, just as if they had
not been regenerated in the lustral waters of the uprising.
But it will not take long for revolutionary Germany to
receive a more significant and sterner lesson in this regard,
for it will be administered to it from nearer at hand. Indeed,
no one thought that by smashing or enfeebling all the ancient
authority, that by stirring up the whole political order of
this country to its depths, the most formidable complications,
a question of life and death for Germany's future would be
aroused—the racial question. They forgot that there are in
the very heart of this Germany whose unity is dreamed of,
in the Bohemian basin and in the Slavic lands surrounding it,
six to seven million men for whom, generation after generation, Germany for centuries has not one instant ceased to be
something worse than a foreigner, for whom the German is
always a *Nemets*. Of course, it is not a matter here of the
literary patriotism of some Prague scholars, honorable as they
may be; these men have doubtless given great service to the
cause of their country, and they will give it more; but that
is not where the life of Bohemia is.[29] The life of a people is
never in the books printed for it, unless it be the German
people; the life of a people is in its instincts and in its beliefs,
and books—it must be admitted—do more to enervate and
sully them than to cheer and support them. All that remains
to Bohemia, thus, of true national life is its *Hussite* beliefs,[30]
in that always living protest of its oppressed Slav nationality
against the usurpation of the Roman Church as well as
against the German rule. That is the bond which makes it
one with all its past of struggles and glory; and that is also
the link which will one day reconnect the *Czech* of Bohemia
with his brothers of the East. We cannot insist too much on
this point, for it is precisely on these sympathetic memories
of the Church of the East, it is on these returns to the *old
faith*, of which Hussitism in its time was only an imperfect
and distorted expression, that a profound difference between
Poland and Bohemia is based: between Bohemia submitting
to the yoke of Western society only despite itself and se-

[29] See above, "To Hanka" and both poems entitled "To the Slavs."
[30] See above, "Hus at the Stake."

183

ditiously Catholic Poland—fanatic partisan of the West and constant traitor to its own.

I know that for the moment the real question in Bohemia is still not posed and what is in movement and rising to the surface of the country is the most vulgar liberalism, mixed with communism in the cities and probably with a little Jacobinism in the countryside. But all this intoxication will soon fall, and at the rate things are going the main point of the situation will soon appear. Then the question for Bohemia will be the following: once the Austrian Empire has disintegrated through the loss of Lombardy and through the now complete emancipation of Hungary,[31] what will Bohemia do with these peoples surrounding it, Moravians, Slovaks, that is to say, seven to eight million men of the same language and race as it? Will it try to set itself up in an independent fashion, or will it favor entering the ridiculous design of that future Germanic Union, which will never be anything more than a Union of Chaos?[32] It is hardly probable that this last course tempts it much. From that moment on it will infallibly be exposed to all sorts of enmities and assaults and it certainly is not on Hungary that it will be able to lean for support in resisting them. Thus, in order to know towards what power Bohemia, despite the ideas which dominate her today and the institutions which will govern her tomorrow, will perforce be drawn, I need only recall what the most nationalist of the patriots of this country said to me in 1841 in Prague. "Bohemia," Hanka said to me, "will be free and independent, will really be in possession of itself, only on the day that Russia comes into possession of Galicia." It is generally worthy of note that this stubborn preference for Russia, the Russian name, her glory, her future, is still met among nationalists of Prague; and this is at the very moment that our faithful ally, Germany, was becoming, with more disinterestedness than justice, the understudy of the Polish emigration, in order to rouse the public opinion of all Europe against us. Every Russian who has visited Prague in the course of these last years can certify that the only

[31] In March 1848, one month before Tyutchev's article, the Hungarians were granted an independent ministry by the Austrians. One year later, Hungary declared its independence, but was soon suppressed.

[32] The answer was given after the first World War, of course, with the formation of Czechoslovakia.

complaint he has heard against us is that of the reserve and indifference with which the national sympathies of Bohemia were received among us. Lofty, generous motives imposed that conduct upon us; now, assuredly, this would be no more than a misunderstanding: for the sacrifices we then made to the cause of order we could henceforth make only to the advantage of the Revolution.

But if it is true that Russia in present circumstances has less than ever the right to discourage sympathies that might come to her, it is fair to recognize, on the other hand, that an historic law has up till now providentially governed her destinies: it is always her most embittered enemies that have worked with most success for the growth of her greatness. This providential law has just raised up one who will certainly play a great part in her future destinies and will more than moderately contribute to accelerating their fulfillment. This enemy is Hungary. I mean Magyar Hungary. Of all Russia's enemies it is perhaps this one which hates her with the most furious hatred. The Magyar people, in whom the revolutionary fervor has been blended by the strangest of combinations with the savagery of an Asiatic horde, of whom it could be said with as much justice as of the Turks that it is only pitching its tent in Europe, lives surrounded by Slavic peoples all of whom are equally loathsome to it. A personal enemy of this race whose destinies it has for so long undermined, it is again imprisoned in the middle of it after centuries of disturbance and tumult. All these people who surround it—Serbs, Croats, Slovaks, Transylvanians, and even the Little Russians of the Carpathians—are the links of a chain it thought forever broken. And now it feels over it a hand which can, whenever it pleases, rejoin these links and tighten the chain again at will. This is the reason for its instinctive hatred of Russia. On the other hand, because of their faith in foreign journalism, the present leaders of the party are seriously persuaded that the Magyar people had a great mission to fulfill in the Orthodox East; that it was up to it, in short, to hold the destinies of Russia in check. So far the moderating authority of Austria had more or less restrained all this unruliness and irrationality; but now that the last bond has been broken and it is the poor old father, sunk into dotage, who has been put in guardianship, it may be predicted that completely emancipated Magyarism is going to give free rein to all these eccentricities and under-

185

take the maddest adventures. There has already been a question of the permanent incorporation of Transylvania. There is talk of reviving ancient rights over the principalities of the Danube and over Serbia. Propaganda in all these countries to stir them up against Russia is going to be redoubled, and when confusion is everywhere, we can count on them one fine day appearing in arms in order to reclaim, in the name of the West whose rights were encroached upon, possession of the mouths of the Danube. And in a haughty voice they will say to Russia, "You will go no further."[33] Those are certainly a few of the articles of the program now being elaborated at Pressburg. Last year it was still all only phrases in a newspaper, now it can at any moment be expressed by very serious and very dangerous attempts. What nevertheless appears most imminent is a conflict between Hungary and the two Slavic realms neighboring upon it. In fact, Croatia and Slovenia, having foreseen that the weakening of legitimate authority at Vienna would unfailingly hand them over to the mercy of Magyarism, have apparently procured for themselves, together with Dalmatia and the military frontier, the promise of a separate organization from the Austrian government. The attitude that these countries thus grouped are trying to take towards Hungary is bound to aggravate all the ancient quarrels and will soon bring about an open civil war; and since the authority of the Austrian government will probably be too weak to intervene between the contending forces with any chance of success, the Slavs of Hungary, who are the weakest, would probably succumb in the struggle, except for one circumstance which must sooner or later unfailingly come to their aid: it is that the enemy whom they are battling is above all the enemy of Russia, and along the whole military frontier, three-quarters of which is made up of Orthodox Serbs, there is not one military guardhouse (according even to Austrian travelers) where, beside the portrait of the Emperor of Austria, one does not find the portrait of another Emperor whom these loyal races insist upon considering the only legitimate one. Besides—why hide it—it is hardly likely that all these earthquake shocks which are overturning the West are stopping

---

[33] One hundred thousand Russian troops did enter Hungary in 1849, at the request of the Austro-Hungarian emperor, to help the Austrians put down the Hungarian rebellion.

at the threshold of the countries of the East; and how, in
this war to the death, in this impious crusade that the Revolution, already mistress of three-quarters of Western Europe,
is preparing against Russia, how could the Christian East,
the Slav-Orthodox East whose life is indissolubly bound to
ours not be behind us in the struggle, and the war may even
begin through it: for we can predict that all the propaganda
that is already at work, Catholic propaganda, revolutionary
propaganda, etc., etc., completely opposed to each other but
at one in a feeling of common hatred against Russia, is now
setting to work with more ardor than ever. We can be certain that they will stop at nothing to gain their ends. And
what, just Heaven, would be the fate of all these populations
of the same Christian faith as we if, exposed as they already
are to all these horrible influences, if the sole authority they
invoke in their prayers should play them false at a time like
this? In short, what would not be the terrible confusion
into which these countries of the East at close quarters with
the Revolution would fall if the legitimate sovereign, if
the Orthodox Emperor of the East for long delayed his
appearance!

No, it is impossible, the forewarnings of a thousand years
are not deceptive. Russia, the country of faith, will not lack
faith at the supreme moment. She will not be frightened of
the splendor of her destiny and will not recoil before her
mission.

And when has this mission been clearer and more obvious?
It can be said that God writes it in letters of fire across a sky
black with storms. The West is on its way, everything is
collapsing, everything is being engulfed in a general conflagration, the Europe of Charlemagne as well as the Europe
of the treaties of 1815; the papacy of Rome and all the royalties of the West; Catholicism and Protestantism; the faith
long lost and reason reduced to absurdity; order henceforth
impossible, liberty henceforth impossible, and on all these
ruins piled up by it, civilization committing suicide.

And when over this huge wreck we see this Empire float
larger than ever, like a Holy Ark, who will doubt her mission;
is it for us, her children, to prove skeptical and fainthearted?

THE ROMAN QUESTION[34] 🔊

If there is one question of the day, or rather the century, that summarizes and, so to speak, focuses all the anomalies, all the contradictions, and all the impossibilities against which Western Europe is struggling, it surely is the Roman question.

And it could not be otherwise, thanks to that inexorable logic which God has put like a hidden justice into the events of the world. The deep and irreconcilable split which tormented the West for centuries finally had to find its supreme expression, it had to penetrate to the root of the tree. Now, no one will dispute this title to fame with Rome: it is still in our time, as it has always been, the root of the Western world. It is nevertheless doubtful, despite the lively discussion this question has aroused, that anyone is really aware of what it involves.

What probably contributes to the lack of understanding of the nature and scope of the question is, first, the false analogy of what we have seen happen in Rome with the past record of its prior revolutions; second, it is the very real community of interests which binds the present movement in Rome[35] to the general movement of the European Revolution. All those additional circumstances which at first sight appear to explain the Roman question in reality only serve to conceal its depth.

No, certainly, this question is not like any other—for not only does it touch upon everything in the West; it could even be said that it goes beyond it.

We assuredly would not be accused of paradox or of spreading slander when we assert that at the present time everything that still remains of actual Christianity in the West is connected, either explicitly or by more or less acknowledged relationships, with Roman Catholicism, whose papacy, as the centuries have made it, is obviously its keystone and necessary condition of existence.

---

[34] Written in October 1849, "The Roman Question" was published in the issue of *La Revue des deux mondes* for January 1850.

[35] The movement for Italian unity and independence, which involved the demand that the Papal States cease to exist as a separate state but be incorporated into the Italian nation. This is what finally happened, of course, when Italy was unified in 1870 (with the exception of Vatican City itself).

Protestantism with its numerous branches, after having
barely lived through three centuries, is dying of decrepitude
in all the countries where it has prevailed until now, England
alone excepted; or, if it does still show some traces of life,
these traces aspire to rejoin Rome. As for the religious doctrines brought forth outside all communion with one or the
other of these two creeds, they are obviously only individual
opinions.

In short, the papacy—this is the sole pillar which in the
West somehow supports whatever bit of the Christian edifice
is still standing after the great destruction of the sixteenth
century and the successive collapses which have taken place
since. Now it is the base of this pillar that they are preparing
to attack.[36]

We are very well acquainted with the platitudes, both in
the daily press and in the official statements of some governments, which are habitually used to mask reality: No one
wants to touch the religious institution of the papacy; every-
body is on his knees before it; it is respected, it is supported;
no one even disputes the papacy's temporal authority—it is
just a matter of modifying the exercise of that authority.
Only concessions recognized to be absolutely necessary are
asked of it and only perfectly legitimate reforms will be imposed upon it. There is in all this a medium amount of bad
faith and a superabundance of illusions.

There is certainly some bad faith, even on the part of the
most ingenuous, in pretending to believe that serious and
sincere reforms introduced into the present government of
the Roman state could avoid resulting after a time in a complete secularization of that state.

But the question is not even that: the real question is to
whose advantage this secularization would be, that is, what
would be the nature, the spirit, and the propensities of the
power to whom you would give temporal authority after
having taken it away from the papacy? For—you cannot
ignore it—it is under the tutelage of this new power that the
papacy would henceforth be destined to live.

It is here that illusions abound. We know the fetishism of
Westerners for everything that is form, formula, and political
structure. This fetishism has become a kind of last religion of
the West; but unless you have your eyes and mind com-

[36] That is, the religious base of the papacy as well as its secular power.

pletely closed and sealed to all experience as to all evidence, how, after what has just happened, can you still persuade yourself that in the present state of Europe, of Italy, of Rome, the liberal or semi-liberal institutions that you will have prescribed for the pope would long remain in the hands of that middle, moderate, mitigated opinion that you are pleased to dream of in the interest of your thesis, that they would not promptly be overrun by the Revolution and soon converted into war machines to attack not only the temporal sovereignty of the pope, but the religious institution itself? For while you may have instructed the revolutionary principle as the Eternal did Satan to molest only the body of Job without touching his soul, be well convinced that the Revolution, less scrupulous than the angel of darkness, will take no notice of your injunctions.

All illusion, all misunderstanding in this regard is impossible for one who has really comprehended the basis of the struggle agitating the West—which centuries ago became its very life, an abnormal but real life, a sickness which does not date from yesterday and is constantly progressing. And if he meets so few men who are aware of this situation, that only proves the sickness is already far advanced.

There is no doubt, so far as the Roman question is concerned, that most of the interests demanding reforms and concessions from the pope are honest, legitimate interests with no ulterior motives; and that satisfaction is due them, and even that it can no longer be denied them. Still the incredible, but inevitable, fortune of the situation is such that these interests, of a purely local nature and of comparatively minor value, control and compromise a huge question. These are the unassuming and harmless dwellings of private persons so situated that they command a fortress, and unfortunately the enemy is at the gates.

For once again, secularization of the Roman state is the aim of all the sincere and serious reform they would like to introduce, and on the other hand, secularization in present circumstances would only be disarming before the enemy—capitulation.

Well, what is there to say? That the Roman question posed in these terms is plainly a labyrinth with no exit; that the papal institution, because of the growth of a hidden imperfection, has arrived, after lasting some centuries, at that period of existence in which life, as is said, is only felt be-

cause of the obstacles to its being; that Rome, which made
the West in its image, is driven into a corner by it? We do
not say the contrary.

Here, as manifest as the sun, blazes that Providential logic
which rules the events of this world like an inner law.

Soon eight centuries will have gone by since the day that
Rome broke the last bond that attached it to the Orthodox
tradition of the Universal Church. By setting itself a separate
destiny Rome on that day decided the destiny of the West
for centuries.

The dogmatic differences which separate Rome from the
Orthodox Church are widely known. From the point of
view of human reason, this difference, while causing the
separation, does not sufficiently explain the chasm which has
been dug, not between the two Churches—since the Church
is One and Universal—but between the two worlds, between
the two humanities, so to speak, who have followed these
two different flags.

It does not sufficiently explain how what turned aside then
had necessarily to end in the position in which we see it
today.

Jesus Christ had said, "My Kingdom is not of this world."
Well, it is a matter of understanding how Rome, after separating itself from the Oneness, believed it had the right, in
an interest which it identified with the interest of Christianity itself, to set up a Kingdom of Christ as a kingdom of this
world.

We are well aware that it is very difficult to give this saying its legitimate meaning in the ideas of the West; one will
always be tempted to explain it, not in the Orthodox sense,
but in a Protestant sense. However, the distance between
these two senses is the distance that separates the divine from
the human. But it must be admitted that this immeasurable
distance only exists because the Orthodox doctrine is hardly
more conciliatory than that of Rome—and this is why:

It is true that Rome has not done the same thing as Protestantism, it has not abolished the Christian focal point which
is the Church to the advantage of the human ego—but it did
absorb it in the Roman ego. It did not deny the tradition, it
was satisfied with confiscating it for its own advantage. But
is not usurpation of the divine the same as its denial? And
that is what sets up that formidable but indisputable solidarity which through time attaches the origin of Protestantism

191

to the usurpations of Rome. For usurpation is peculiar not only in that it instigates rebellion, but in that it creates an appearance of right for its own advantage.

The modern Revolutionary school is not fooled. The Revolution, which is only the apotheosis of this same human ego come to its total and full flowering, has not failed to acknowledge as its own and to hail as its two glorious masters Luther as well as Gregory VII.[37] A kindred voice has spoken to it and it has adopted the former despite his Christian beliefs, while it has almost canonized the latter, pope though he was.[38]

But if the obvious relation which binds the three terms of this series is the very basis of the historical life of the West, it is also indisputable that the relation can have no other origin than the profound alteration which Rome forced upon the Christian principle by the organization it imposed upon it.

In the course of centuries the Church of the West, under the patronage of Rome, has almost entirely lost the character which the law of its origin had assigned it. It ceased to be a society of the faithful freely united in spirit and truth under the law of Christ in the midst of the great human society. It became an institution, a political power—a State within a State. To tell the truth, all through the Middle Ages the Church in the West was nothing but a Roman colony set up in a conquered country.

It is this organization which, by attaching the Church to the soil of terrestrial interests, has made it, so to speak, mortally destined. By embodying the divine element in a frail and perishable body, it has made it liable to all the frailties as well as to all the appetites of the flesh. By Providential fortune, this organization brought to the Roman Church the necessity for war, for earthly war, a necessity which was equivalent to absolute condemnation for an institution like the Church. Of this organization was born the conflict of claims and rivalry of interests which could but result in a fierce struggle between the papacy and the empire—and this

[37] Pope from 1073 to 1085, Gregory was one of the strongest popes in the struggle against the Holy Roman Empire. He it was who humiliated Henry IV at Canossa. Incidentally, it was under Gregory that celibacy of the Roman Catholic priesthood was introduced.

[38] Because of Gregory's victory over the Empire.

truly impious and sacrilegious duel prolonged all through
the Middle Ages mortally wounded the very principle of
authority in the West.

This is the cause of so much excess, violence, heinous
crimes, piled up for centuries in order to shore up this material power which Rome believed necessary to safeguard
the unity of the Church, but they nevertheless ended, as they
had to end, by shattering this alleged unity. For it cannot be
denied, the explosion of the Reformation in the sixteenth
century was originally only the reaction of the too-long
offended Christian consciousness against the authority of a
Church which in many ways was no longer so but in name.
But since for centuries Rome had carefully come between the
Universal Church and the West, the heads of the Reformation, instead of taking their complaints to the tribunal of the
legitimate and competent authority,[39] preferred to summon
them to the judgment of the individual conscience—that is
to say, they made themselves judges in their own cause.

This is the rock upon which the reform of the sixteenth
century foundered. With all due respect to the scholars of the
West, such is the real and only cause for the deviation of this
movement of reform—Christian in origin, it ended in negation of the authority of the Church, and consequently, of
the very principle of all authority. And it is through this
breach that Protestantism opened, so to speak unknown to
itself, that the anti-Christian principle later erupted into the
society of the West.

This result was inevitable, for the human ego left to itself
is anti-Christian in essence. The rebellion, the usurpation of
the ego, assuredly does not date from the last three centuries,
but what was new then, what happened for the first time in
the history of mankind was that this rebellion, this usurpation
was raised to the dignity of a principle and acted in the name
of a right essentially inherent in the human personality.

Just as the absence of Christianity in the world was necessary for man to be inspired to such proud claims, so the
absence of a legitimate sovereign was necessary to make the
rebellion complete and the usurpation flagrant.

For these last three centuries the historical life of the West
thus has not been, and could not be, anything but a constant
war, a continual assault upon all Christian elements in the

[39] That is, to the Orthodox Church.

composition of ancient Western society. This work of de-
molition has been long, for before being able to attack the
institutions, it was necessary to destroy the cement which
held them together, that is, the beliefs.

What made the first French Revolution a date forever
memorable in the history of the world is that it inaugurated,
so to speak, the advent of the anti-Christian idea to the
governments of the political society.

To convince oneself that this idea is characteristic and by
way of the soul itself of the Revolution, it is enough to
examine its essential dogma—the new dogma it has brought
to the world. This is obviously the dogma of the sovereignty
of the people. Now, what is the sovereignty of the people if
not the human ego multiplied by the people's number—that
is, supported by force? Everything that is not this principle is
no longer the Revolution and can have only a purely relative
and contingent value. That is why, be it said in passing,
nothing is more nonsensical, or more perfidious, than to
attribute any other value to the political institutions the
Revolution has created. These are devices of war admirably
suited to the employment for which they were designed, but
aside from this object, totally unfit for any use in an orderly
society.

Besides, the Revolution has itself taken care to leave us
in no doubt of its real nature by thus formulating its relation
to Christianity: "The State as such has no religion." For such
is the creed of the modern State.

To tell the truth, that is the great innovation the Revolution has brought to the world. That is its own, essential
work—a deed without precedent in the history of human
societies.

This was the first time a political society had agreed to the
administration of a State completely alien to all approbation
superior to man; a State which declared it had no soul, or if
it had one, this soul was not religious. For who does not
know that even in pagan antiquity, in all that world on the
other side of the cross, placed under the empire of the universal tradition that paganism could distort but not interrupt—
the city, the State was above all a religious institution. It was
like an isolated fragment of the universal tradition which,
embodied in a particular society, formed a kind of self-
contained center. This was, so to speak, localized, materialized
religion.

We know quite well that this alleged neutrality in religious matters is not serious on the part of the Revolution. It is too well aware of the nature of its adversary not to know that neutrality in regard to it is impossible. "Who is not with me is against me." In fact, in order to offer neutrality to Christianity, one must no longer be a Christian. The sophistry of the modern doctrine here founders on the all-powerful nature of facts. In order for this alleged neutrality to make sense, in order for it to be something other than a snare and a delusion, it would be necessary for the modern State to agree to strip itself of all features of moral authority, to submit to being only a simple police institution, a simple, earthly fact, by nature incapable of expressing any moral idea whatsoever. Will anyone seriously maintain that the Revolution would accept a condition like this for the State it has created and which represents it, a not only lowly, but impossible condition? It would so little accept it that, according to its well-known doctrine, it derives the incompetence of modern law in religious matters only from its conviction that morality stripped of all supernatural sanction is sufficient for the destinies of human society. This proposition could be true or false, but this proposition, we claim, is a complete doctrine, and for every man of good faith, a doctrine equivalent to the most complete negation of Christian truth.

Also, despite this alleged incompetence and constitutional neutrality in matters of religion, we see that everywhere that the modern State has been set up it has not failed to demand and to exercise the same authority and the same rights towards the Church as those which belonged to the earlier authorities. Thus, in France, for example, in this preeminent country of logic, the law is careful to declare that the State as such has no religion; but the State no less persists, in its relations with the Catholic Church, upon regarding itself as the perfectly legitimate heir of the most Christian King, the eldest son of this Church.

Let us, then, restore truth on the basis of facts. The modern State only prohibits State religions because it has its own—and this religion is the Revolution. Now, to return to the Roman question, we can easily understand the impossible position they are putting the papacy in by obliging it to accept the conditions of the modern State for its temporal sovereignty. The papacy knows very well the nature of the principle being extolled. It understands it instinctively, the

195

Christian conscience of the priest in the pope would warn
him of it in an emergency. There is no possible dealing
between the papacy and this principle; for dealing would not
be a mere concession of power, it would be plain apostasy.
But, it will be said, why should not the pope accept the
institutions without the principle? That is one of the illusions
of so-called moderate opinion, which believes itself eminently
reasonable, and is only obtuse. As if institutions could be
separated from the principle that created them and gave them
life. As if the material body of institutions deprived of their
soul were anything but a dead and useless apparatus—just
rubbish. Besides, political institutions always finally have the
meaning attributed to them not by those who get them, but
by those who grant them—above all when they assign them
to you.

If the pope had been only a priest, that is, if the papacy had
remained loyal to its origin, the Revolution would not have
had any hold over it, for the persecution of it is not one. But
it is the mortal and perishable element with which it identified
itself that has now made it vulnerable to persecution's blows.
That is the pawn which the Roman papacy centuries ago, in
advance, gave to the Revolution.

It is here, as we have said, that the sovereign logic of
Providential action is blindingly manifested. Of all the institutions the papacy has given birth to since its separation
from the Orthodox Church, the one which has most deeply
marked this separation, which has most increased it, most
strengthened it, without doubt is the sovereignty of the pope.
And it is exactly this institution that we see the papacy butting
against today.

It is certainly a long time since the world has had anything
comparable to the spectacle proffered by unhappy Italy during
those final days which preceded its new disasters. It is a long
time since any situation, any historical fact has had this strange
aspect. It sometimes happens that individuals on the verge of
some great misfortune are apparently for no reason suddenly
overcome by a fit of frantic gaiety, of furious hilarity—well,
this whole people was suddenly seized by a fit of this nature.
And this fever, this delirium was kept up, was spread for
months. There was one moment when it enfolded all classes,
all conditions of society like an electric cable, and this delirium,
so intense, so general, adopted as its slogan the name of a
pope!

How many times was the poor Christian priest in the
depths of his retreat not obliged to tremble at the noise of
this orgy of which he was made the god! How many times
did these declarations of love, these convulsions of rapture
not bring dismay and doubt to the soul of this Christian
given for a prey to this frightening popularity!

What should have dismayed the pope above all is that
beneath this enormous popularity, through all this exaltation
of the masses, however unbridled it was, he could not mistake
calculation and hidden motive.

This was the first time that the pope, as distinct from the
papacy, was set apart for adoration. It is not enough to say
that all these tributes, all these adorations were addressed to
the man only because it was hoped he would betray the
institution. In short, the aim was to celebrate the pope while
making a bonfire of the papacy. And what was particularly
dangerous in this situation is that this calculation, this hidden
motive was not only part of the design of the parties, it was
also part of the instinctive feeling of the masses. And assuredly
nothing could better bare all the falsity and all the hypocrisy
of the situation than the apotheosis bestowed upon the head
of the Catholic Church at the very moment that a more
ardent persecution than ever was let loose against the Jesuits.

The institution of the Jesuits will always be a problem for
the West. It is still one of those puzzles whose key is missing.
It can truly be said that the question of the Jesuits is too close
to the West's religious conscience for it ever to be resolved
in an entirely satisfactory way.

When speaking of the Jesuits, when looking for a way to
evaluate them fairly, one must begin by ignoring all those
(and their name is legion) for whom the word Jesuit is no
more than a password, a war-cry. Certainly, of all the apol-
ogies attempted in favor of this order, none is more eloquent,
more convincing than the hatred, that furious and implacable
hatred sworn against it by all enemies of the Christian religion.
But this allowed, we cannot conceal that many most sincere
Roman Catholics, many most devoted to their Church, from
Pascal to our days, continue, generation after generation, to
nourish a declared, unconquerable antipathy for this institution. This state of mind in a large fraction of the Catholic
world constitutes what is perhaps one of the most really
striking and most tragic situations in which it has been given
to the human soul to be placed.

Indeed, what conflict more profoundly tragic could be imagined than that which must arise in the heart of a man when, divided between the feeling of religious veneration, of more than filial piety, and a loathsome fact, he makes every effort to reject, to drive away the testimony of his own conscience rather than acknowledge the real and incontestable interdependence between the object of his worship and that of his detestation? However, such is the situation of every faithful Catholic who, blinded by his hostility for the Jesuits, tries to hide such a shatteringly obvious fact from himself, to wit: the profound, the intimate interdependence which binds this order, its propensities, its doctrines, its destinies, with the propensities, the doctrines, the destinies of the Roman Church, and the absolute impossibility of separating one from the other without producing an organic lesion and obvious mutilation. For if, getting rid of all prejudice, of all bias of party, of sect, and even of nationality, with mind devoted to the most absolute impartiality and heart filled with Christian charity, one should stand before history and reality and, after having examined both of them, should honestly propound this question, what are the Jesuits? this, we think, would be the answer: the Jesuits are men filled with an ardent, tireless, often heroic zeal for the Christian cause who are nevertheless guilty of a great crime against Christianity, which is that, dominated by the human ego, not as individuals, but as an order, they believe the Christian cause so bound to their own—so completely have they, in the ardor of the chase and in the emotion of battle, forgotten these words of the Master: "Thy will be done and not mine" —that they end by seeking the victory of God at any price except that of their personal satisfaction. But this mistake, which has its root in man's original sin and whose consequences have been of incalculable import for the interests of Christianity, is not something special to the Society of Jesus, far from it. It holds this mistake, this propensity, so much in common with the Church of Rome itself that one would be quite correct to say that this it is that attaches them to each other by a truly organic affinity, by a real bond of blood. It is this community, this identity of propensities that makes the institution of the Jesuits the concentrated but literally faithful expression of Roman Catholicism; that makes it, in short, Roman Catholicism itself, but in the state of action, the state militant.

That is why this order—*"tossed about from age to age,"* through persecution and triumph, insult and apotheosis—in the West has never found, and cannot find, either religious convictions sufficiently disinterested in its cause to be able to appraise it, or a religious authority competent to judge it. A portion of Western society, that which has resolutely broken with the Christian principle, has attacked the Jesuits only in order better, under cover of their unpopularity, to strengthen the blows it addresses against its true enemy. As for those Catholics still loyal to Rome who have become opponents of this order, although individually speaking they can as Christians be right, nevertheless as Roman Catholics they are defenseless against it, for when they attack it they constantly expose themselves to the danger of wounding the Roman Church itself.

But it is not only against the Jesuits, that vital strength of Catholicism, that people tried to exploit the half-artificial, half-sincere popularity of Pius IX. Still another party counted on him; another mission was reserved for him.

The partisans of national independence hoped that, by completely secularizing the papacy for the advantage of their causes, he who is a priest above all would agree to become the standard-bearer of Italian liberty. Thus we have the two most deep-rooted and most dominant feelings of contemporary Italy—antipathy for the secular dominion of the clergy and traditional hatred of the foreigner, the barbarian, the German—both for the advantage of their own cause demanding the cooperation of the pope. The whole world glorified him, even deified him, but on condition that he become the servant of the whole world, and that in a sense in no way that of Christian humility.

Among the political opinions or influences which have recently solicited his patronage while offering him their assistance, there was one which had earlier made some splash because it had had some men of rare literary talent as interpreters and apostles. To believe the ingenuously ambitious doctrines of these political theoreticians, contemporary Italy, under the auspices of the Roman pontificate, was going to recover universal primacy and for the third time capture the scepter of the world. That is, at the very moment that the papal establishment was shaken to its foundations they were earnestly proposing to the pope an improvement upon the inheritance of the Middle Ages and were offering him something like a Christian Caliphate, of course on condition that this new theocracy be used above all in the national interests of Italy.

One really cannot marvel enough at this propensity for the chimerical and impossible which dominates the minds of our time and is one of the distinctive features of the age. There had to be a real affinity between utopian ideas and the Revolution, for each time the latter, disloyal for a moment to its custom, wants to create instead of destroy, it unerringly falls into utopian ideas. It is fair to say that the ones we have just alluded to are still among the most inoffensive.

Finally the given situation reached the point that, equivocation no longer being possible, the papacy, in order to recover its right, was obliged to break a lance with the pope's alleged friends. It was then that the Revolution in its turn threw aside its mask and appeared in the world in the lineaments of the Roman republic.

As for this party, we know it now, we have seen it at work. It is the real, the legitimate representative of the Revolution in Italy. This party thinks of the papacy as its personal enemy because of the Christian element it has perceived in it. It would simply like to abolish it, and it is for a like reason that it would also like to abolish all of Italy's past, all the historical conditions of its existence, because they are tainted and polluted by Catholicism, hoping by pure revolutionary abstraction to bind the existence of the government it is claiming to found to the republican antecedents of ancient Rome.

Well, what is special in this savage utopia is that, whatever may be the profoundly anti-historical character with which it is stamped, it also has its well-known tradition in the history of Italian civilization. After all, it is only a classical reminiscence of the ancient pagan world, of pagan civilization—a tradition which has played a great part in the history of Italy, which has been preserved through all the past of this country, which has had its representatives, its heroes, and even its martyrs, and which, not content with almost exclusive domination of its arts and its literature, has many times tried to establish itself politically in order to take over society completely. And it is remarkable that each time this tradition, this propensity has tried to spring up again, it has always appeared like a ghost invariably attached to the same locality —Rome.

When the tradition came down to our days, the revolutionary principle could hardly fail to welcome it and appropriate it, because of the anti-Christian thought in it. Now this party has just been beaten and the authority of the pope has apparently been restored. But it must be admitted that if anything could still swell the wealth of misfortunes that this Roman question comprises, it would be the double effect procured by the intervention of France.[40]

Ordinary current opinion on the subject of this intervention generally sees in it no more than an impulsive act or a blunder by the French government. The real thing to say on this subject is that if the French government, by getting involved in this question insoluble in itself, did not know that it was more insoluble for it than for anyone else, that would only be evidence of complete ignorance on its part, both of its own position and of that of France—which is quite possible, we admit.

Latterly people in Europe are generally too used to summarizing the value of the acts, or rather, of the whims of action of French politics by a now proverbial phrase: "France doesn't know what it wants." That may be true, but to be perfectly correct one should add that France cannot know what it wants. For in order to succeed one must have above all *One* will—and for sixty years France has been doomed to have two.

Here it is not a matter of that disagreement, of that divergence of political or other opinions met in all countries where the course of circumstances has handed society over to government by parties. It is a matter of a quite differently important fact; it is a matter of a permanent, essential, eternally insoluble antagonism which for sixty years has formed, so to speak, the very basis of national consciousness in France. It is the soul of France which is divided.

Since the Revolution got hold of this country it has indeed been able to unsettle it, to modify it, profoundly to change it, but it has not been able, nor will it ever be able, entirely to become one with it. It will try in vain, there are elements, principles in the moral life of France which will always resist —or at least as long as there is a France in the world. They are: the Catholic Church with its beliefs and its teaching;

---

[40] French intervention in Italian affairs continued through the reign of Napoleon III.

Christian marriage and the family; and even property. On
the other hand, we may predict that the Revolution, which
has entered not only into the blood, but into the very soul of
this society, will never bring itself voluntarily to let go its
hold, and since we know no exorcism in the history of the
world applicable to a whole nation, it is much to be feared
that the state of struggle, but of an inward, incessant struggle,
of permanent and, so to speak, organic division, will be the
normal condition of the new French society for quite a long
time to come.

And that is why in this country, where for sixty years we
have seen this combination of a State revolutionary by principle dragging along a society which is only revolutionized,
the government, the authority which necessarily restrains the
two without managing to bring them together, is fatally
doomed to a false, precarious position, surrounded by dangers
and smitten with impotence. We have also seen that since
this epoch all the governments in France—except one, that of
the Convention during the Terror—whatever the differences
of origin, doctrines, and leanings, have had one thing in common: all, not even excepting the one the day after February,
have suffered the Revolution much more than they have
represented it. And it could not be otherwise. For it is only
by struggling against it, even while suffering it, that they
could live. But it is correct to say that up to now at least,
they have all perished at the task.

How, then, could a power thus made, as little sure of its
right, of such an unsettled nature, have any chance of success
when it interferes in a question such as the Roman question?
When it offers itself as a mediator or arbitrator between the
Revolution and the pope, it could hardly hope to reconcile
what is irreconcilable by nature. And on the other hand, it
could not give the victory to one of the opposing parties
without wounding itself, without denying, so to speak, a half
of itself. All it could therefore do by this double-edged inter-
ference, however blunt the edges might be, was to confuse
still more what was already inextricable, to make the wound
worse by irritating it. In this it has perfectly succeeded.

Now, what is the real situation of the pope vis-à-vis his
subjects? And what is the probable fate of the new institutions
he has just accorded them? Unhappily, only the most melancholy predictions are correct. Do not doubt it.

The situation is the same as it has always been, the same as it was just before the present reign, when the government collapsed under the weight of its impossibility, but immeasurably aggravated by everything that has happened since. On the moral side, by the enormous deceits and enormous treacheries; on the material side, by all the accumulated destruction.

We know the vicious circle in which we have for forty years watched so many peoples and so many governments wander and struggle. The governed accepted the concessions given them by the power only as slight instalments reluctantly paid by a debtor in bad faith. The governments saw in the requests addressed to them only the traps of a hypocritical enemy. Well, this situation, this reciprocity of bad feelings, everywhere and always execrable and corrupting, is in this case still more greatly exacerbated by the especially holy character of the authority and by the extraordinary nature of its relations with its subjects. For, once again, in the given situation, on the downward slope where we are placed, not only by men's passions but owing to the very force of circumstances, every concession, every reform, regardless of how serious and sincere it may be, is infallibly pushing the Roman State into complete secularization. There is no doubt that secularization will be the outcome of the situation. Nevertheless, the pope, who has no right to grant it even in ordinary times—since the temporal sovereignty does not belong to him but to the Church of Rome—may even less agree to it now that he is certain that this secularization, even when conceded to real necessities, would definitively result in the advantage of the sworn enemies not only of his authority, but of the Church itself. To agree to it would be to make himself simultaneously guilty of both apostasy and treason. So much for the authority. As for the subjects, it is clear that the deep-rooted antipathy for priestly dominion, which makes up the entire public spirit of the Roman population, will not have been lessened by recent events.

If, on the one hand, a like frame of mind is alone sufficient to abort the most liberal and most honest reforms, on the other hand, the lack of success of these reforms can only infinitely add to the general exasperation, can only confirm public opinion in its hatred for reinstated authority and—*make recruits for the enemy.*

That is certainly a completely wretched situation which has all the features of Providential punishment. For what greater misfortune for a Christian priest can be imagined than for him to be thus fatally invested with a power which he can use only to the detriment of souls and for the ruin of religion! No, truly, this situation is too violent, too much against nature to be prolonged. Punishment or trial, it is impossible that the Roman papacy will long remain imprisoned in this circle of fire without God in His mercy coming to its aid and opening a way to it, a wonderful conclusion, dazzling, unlooked for, or, to put it better, looked for for centuries.

Perhaps the papacy, and the Church subject to its laws, is still separated from that end by many tribulations and many disasters; perhaps it is only at the beginning of calamitous times. For this will not be a little flame, nor will be the conflagration be brief which, consuming and reducing to ashes whole centuries of worldly concerns and anti-Christian enmities, will finally make the fatal barrier that concealed the longed-for end crumble before it.

How, in view of what is happening, in the face of this new organization of the principle of evil, the cleverest and most fearsome men have ever seen, in the face of this world of evil ready and armed, with its church of irreligion and government of rebellion, how, we say, can Christians be forbidden to hope that God will deign to adjust the forces of His Church to the new task He has assigned it?—that on the eve of the battles being readied He will deign to restore to it the fullness of its powers, and to this end will Himself come in His time, with His merciful hand to heal the wound in the side of His Church that the hands of men did make—that open wound which has been bleeding for eight hundred years!

The Orthodox Church has never despaired of this healing. She awaits it, she relies on it, not with confidence, but with certitude. How could it be that what is *One* in principle, what is *One* in Eternity would not triumph over disunion in time? Despite the separation of many centuries and through all human prejudices, she has not ceased to acknowledge that the Christian principle never perished in the Church of Rome; that it has always been stronger in it than the error and passion of men, and that is why she is inwardly convinced that it will be stronger than all its enemies. She knows, further, that now as for centuries past the Christian destinies of the West are in the hands of the Church of Rome and she hopes that on the day of the great reunion it will return this holy trust whole.

In conclusion, permit us to recall an incident having to do with the visit the Emperor of Russia made to Rome in 1846. Perhaps the general emotion which greeted him at his appearance in St. Peter's is still remembered—the appearance of the Orthodox Emperor returned to Rome after many centuries of absence! and the electric shock that ran through the crowd when they saw him praying at the Tomb of the Apostles! That emotion was right and legitimate. The prostrate Emperor was not alone there. All Russia was prostrated there with him. Let us hope that he will not have prayed before the holy relics in vain.

A LETTER ON THE CENSORSHIP IN RUSSIA[41] ❧

I am taking advantage of the warrant you have been kind
enough to give me to submit some reflections connected
with the subject of our last discussion to you. I surely need
not again express my sympathetic adherence to the idea you
had the goodness to impart to me, and, if there should be an
attempt to realize it, to assure you of my earnest desire to
serve with all means in my power. But it is precisely in order
to be in a better position to do so that I believe it my duty,
first, frankly to explain to you how I see the question. Of
course, it is not a matter here of making a profession of political faith. That would be childish: in our time all reasonable people are pretty much agreed so far as political opinions
are concerned;[42] they differ from each other only by the
greater or lesser degree of intelligence brought to the proper
recognition of what is and to the proper estimation of what
should be. It is on the greater or lesser degree of truth in the
estimations that it is a matter, above all, of understanding
each other. For if it is true, as you have said, my Prince, that
in any given situation a practical mind could only want what
is realizable, due allowance being made for individuals, it is
also true that it would be unworthy of a really practical mind
to want anything whatsoever outside the natural conditions
of its existence. But let us come to the point. If there is one
truth, among many, which has emerged perfectly plainly
from the harsh experience of recent years, it is surely this:
it has been sternly proven to us that a restraint, a too absolute,
too prolonged repression cannot be imposed on intellects
without resulting in serious damage to the whole social
organism. It appears that every weakening, every serious
lessening of intellectual life in a society necessarily results in
the gain of material appetites and sordidly egoistic instincts.
The authority itself in the long run does not escape the dis-
advantages of a like system. A desert, a huge intellectual void

[41] Written in November 1857, this letter was addressed to Prince M. D.
Gorchakov, Nesselrode's successor on the Council of the Empire. According
to Gregg, the letter " . . . was not only well received . . . but earned [Tyutchev]
an appointment as president of the Committee of Foreign Censorship" (Gregg,
Fedor Tiutchev, 17). Gregg gives no authority for his statement. The letter
was printed in Russian translation in 1873. See above, "To Gorchakov."

[42] That is, both Westernizers and Slavophiles were pretty well agreed
on the coming reforms of Alexander II.

develops around the sphere in which he lives, and the guiding
thought, finding outside itself neither check, nor sign, nor
any point of support whatsoever, ends by becoming blurred
and sinking under its own weight, even before succumbing
to the force of events. Fortunately, this stern lesson has not
been lost. The clear judgment and generous nature of the
reigning Emperor[43] understood that it was time to relax the
inordinate severity of the former system and to give intellects
the air they lacked. Well—I say this with complete conviction—whoever has since then followed the totality of the
work produced in the literary movement of the country
must be pleased with the happy effects of this change of
system. No more than another do I shut my eyes to the weak
aspects and sometimes even the errors of the literature of the
day; but there is one merit which cannot be denied it without injustice, and this merit is very real; it is that since the
day a certain measure of freedom of speech was given it, it
has constantly striven its best and as loyally as possible to
express the thought of the country. To a very lively feeling
for contemporary reality and to an often extremely remarkable talent for reproducing it, it has joined a no less lively
solicitude for all the real needs, for all the concerns, for all
the sores of Russian society. Like the country itself which
was faced with improvements to carry out, it was concerned
only with those which were possible, practical, and clearly
indicated, without letting itself be overrun by that so eminently literary disease, utopian ideas. If in the war it has
carried on against corruption it has sometimes allowed itself
to drag in obvious exaggerations, it could be said to its credit
that in its zeal to battle with them its thought has never
separated the interests of the Supreme Authority from those
of the country, so imbued was it with the earnest and loyal
conviction that to war with corruption was to war with the
personal enemies of the Emperor. It has often happened that
in our time similar things under the cloak of zeal have—I am
well aware of it—covered very bad feelings and served to hide
propensities which were nothing less than disloyal; but,
thanks to the experience that men of our age necessarily had
to acquire, nothing is easier than immediately to recognize

---

[43] Alexander II, who had come to the throne in 1855 upon the death of
Nicholas I.

these tricks of the trade and falsities of this kind no longer
fool anyone.

It can be asserted that right now there are in Russia two
dominant feelings which are almost always closely linked:
annoyance or disgust aroused at the persistence of corruption; and a religious confidence in the pure, honest, and benevolent purposes of the sovereign.

There is a general conviction that no one suffers from
Russia's sores more than he and more strenuously longs for
their cure; but perhaps nowhere is this conviction so lively
and so complete as precisely in the class of men of letters, and
it is the fulfillment of a man of honor's duty to seize every
occasion to declare aloud that at this moment there is perhaps
no class of society more piously devoted to the person of the
Emperor.

These judgments—I do not hide it—might well meet more
than one skeptic in some areas of our official world. That
world has always had a kind of suspicious and bad-tempered
party, which is very well explained by their particular point
of view. There are men who know of literature only what
the police of large cities know of the people they keep an eye
on, that is, the improprieties and disorders in which good
people sometimes allow themselves to be involved.

No, whatever is said, so far the government has had no
cause to repent of having relaxed the severity of the system
which weighed upon the press. But was this all that had to be
done in the question of the press; in view of this work of
freer minds and in proportion as the literary movement
grows, will not the usefulness and necessity for higher guidance every day come closer to home? The censorship alone,
however it is exercised, is far from enough for the demands
of the new situation. Censorship is a limit, not a guide. But
among us, in literature as in everything, it is a matter less
of repressing than of guiding. A guide, a strong, intelligent
guide, sure of itself, that is the country's cry, that is the slogan
of our entire situation.

There is often complaint of the spirit of intractability and
insubordination that characterizes the men of the new generation. There is a good deal of misunderstanding in this
accusation. What is certain is that no other age has had so
many active intellects available and champing at the bit of
inertia imposed on them. But these same intellects, from
among whom enemies of authority are recruited, quite often

ask no more than to follow him, the moment he shows himself willing to associate them with his actions and resolutely march at their head. It is this finally recognized truth of experience that has contributed much in different countries perceptibly to modify the relations of the authority with the press since the last revolutionary crises in Europe. And here, my Prince, I will take the liberty of summoning the testimony of your own memories in support of my thesis.

You, who like me knew Germany before 1848, you should recall what the attitude of the press to the German governments then was, what bitterness, what hostility characterized its relations with them, what worries and anxieties it aroused for them.

Well, how has it come about that now these spiteful states of mind have in large part disappeared and been replaced by essentially different states of mind?

It is because today these same governments, who thought of the press as a necessary evil they had to suffer even while abhorring it, have made up their minds to seek an auxiliary force in it and avail themselves of it as of an instrument fitted to their use. I cite this example only to prove that even in countries already strongly penetrated by the Revolution an intelligent and vigorous guide always finds minds prepared to accept and follow him. At any rate, when it is a matter of our concerns, I as much as anyone hate all those alleged analogies people seek abroad; almost always but half understood, they have done us too much harm for me to be prepared to appeal to their authority.

Among us, thank Heaven, there are completely different instincts, completely different demands that must be satisfied; there are other convictions, convictions less shaken and more disinterested which would heed the call of the authority.

In fact, despite the infirmities that afflict us and the vices that deform us, still in our souls (it cannot be too often repeated) there is a wealth of intelligent good will and of dedicated spirit of activity which only await their delivery by sympathetic hands which can recognize and welcome them. In short, if it is true, as has often been said, that the State as well as the Church is entrusted with souls, nowhere is this truth more manifest than in Russia, and also nowhere, it must be allowed, has this mission of the State been easier to exercise and fulfill. So it is with a satisfaction, a unanimous approval, that we would see the authority among us, in its relations with the press, take upon itself the guidance of the honest and loyal public spirit and claim its right to the governance of intellects.

But, my Prince, since I am not writing a semiofficial article at the moment, and since in a confidential and honest letter nothing would be more laughably out of place than circumlocution and reserve, I will try my best to explain as best I can under what conditions, in my opinion, the authority could claim to exercise a similar influence over minds.

First, the country must be taken as it is right now, handed over to very painful, very legitimate mental concerns, between a past filled with teachings, it is true, but also with very discouraging experiences, and a future filled with problems.

Then, with regard to this country, people must realize what parents who see their children growing under their eyes have so much difficulty in acknowledging—an age comes when thought is adult and wants to be treated as such. But in order to gain this moral ascendancy over intellects which have reached the age of reason, without which one cannot claim to guide them, they must above all be given the certitude that in the lofty regions of the authority there are, if not ready-made solutions for all the great questions which concern and impassion the country right now, at least strongly agreed-upon convictions and a body of doctrine all of whose parts are bound together and which is consistent in itself.

No, certainly, it is not a matter of authorizing the public to intervene in the deliberations of the Council of the Empire, nor of having the program of governmental measures meet the press halfway. But what would be essential is that the authority itself be sufficiently convinced of its own ideas, sufficiently imbued with its own convictions to feel the need to spread their influence abroad, and to make it penetrate, like an element of regeneration, like a new life, into the depths of the national consciousness. What would be essential in the face of the crushing difficulties weighing upon us would be for it to understand that without this intimate communication with the very soul of the country, without the full and complete awakening of all these moral and intellectual forces, without their spontaneous and unanimous collaboration in the common work, the government, reduced to its own forces, can do nothing, no more without than within, no more for its welfare than for ours.

In short, all of us, private and official, must not stop telling ourselves and repeating to ourselves that the destinies of Russia are like a vessel run aground, that all the efforts of its crew will never succeed in freeing it, and that only the rising tide of national life will succeed in raising it and putting it afloat.

It is in the name of that principle and of that sentiment that in my opinion the authority could right now take hold of souls and intellects, that it could, so to speak, take them in its hand and carry them wherever it thinks right. They would follow that banner everywhere.

Needless to say, I in no way intend by this to make the government a preacher, to have it mount the pulpit and spout sermons to a silent audience. It is its spirit and not its word that it ought to put into the loyal propaganda that would be done under its auspices.

Since the first condition of success, when one wants to to persuade people, is to be heard by them, it is understood that this healthy propaganda, in order to be received, far from limiting freedom of discussion, on the contrary allows it to be as frank and honest as the circumstances of the country permit.

For it is necessary to insist for the thousandth time on a fact whose obviousness is as evident as the following: in our days, whenever there is not a sufficient measure of freedom of discussion nothing is possible, but absolutely nothing, morally and intellectually speaking. I know how difficult (if not to say impossible) it is in these matters to give one's thought the necessary degree of precision. For example, how can one define what he means by a sufficient measure of freedom in matters of discussion? This measure, essentially fluctuating and arbitrary, is often determined only by what is most deep-rooted and most personal in our convictions; it would be necessary to know everything, so to speak, about the man in order to know the exact sense he attaches to his words when speaking on these questions. For my part, for thirty years I, like so many others, have followed this insoluble question of the press through all the mutabilities of its fortune, and do me the justice to believe, my Prince, that after such a long time of study and observation this question can be for me only the object of the most impartial and coolest evaluation. I have therefore no part, nor prejudice, in anything connected with it; I have not even any marked

animus against the censorship, even though it has latterly
weighed on Russia like a real public calamity. While ad-
mitting its expediency and its relative usefulness, my principal complaint against it is that it is, so far as I can see, profoundly inadequate at the present moment to our true needs
and our true interests. Besides, the question is not one of the
dead letter of rules and directions which have no value apart
from the spirit animating them. The question is entirely one
of the way the government itself, in its heart of hearts, thinks
of its relations with the press; it is, when all is said, in the
greater or lesser legitimacy it accords to the right of individual thought.

And now, to have done with generalities once and for all
and to come more closely to grips with the situation of the
moment, permit me, my Prince, to tell you, with all the
candor of a completely confidential letter, that so long as our
government has not, in its customary thought, fundamentally
modified its way of viewing its relations with the press, so
long as it has not, so to speak, cut all that short, nothing
serious, nothing really effective can be attempted with any
chance of success; and the hope of gaining an ascendancy
over minds by means of a press thus administered will never
be anything but an illusion.

Nevertheless, courage is necessary to view the question
as it is, as circumstances have made it. It is impossible that
the government not be very seriously concerned with something that has been going on for several years and is tending
to take a direction whose impact and consequences no one
can at present foresee. You understand, my Prince, that I
mean the establishment of Russian presses abroad, outside
all control of our government. The fact is assuredly important, very important, and deserves the most serious attention.
It would be useless to try to conceal the progress already
made by this literary propaganda. We know that right now
Russia is flooded with these publications, that they are avidly
sought after, that they pass from hand to hand with a great
ease of circulation, and that they have already penetrated, if
not the masses, who do not read, at least the lower strata of
society. On the other hand, it must be owned that without
having recourse to positively vexatious and tyrannical measures, it would be most difficult effectively to thwart either
the importation and sale of this printed matter or the expor-
tation abroad of manuscripts intended to feed it. Well, let

us have the courage to acknowledge the true import, the true significance of this fact: it has plainly come about because of suppression by the censorship, but suppression by the censorship that redounds to the advantage of a bad and inimical influence; in order to be in a better position to fight this influence, let us try to give an account of whence it derives its strength and to what it owes its success.

Up to now, so far as the Russian press abroad is concerned, the question can of course be only of Herzen's journal.[44] So what is the significance of Herzen for Russia? Who reads him? Is it by any chance utopian socialists and revolutionary leaders who recommend him to one's attention? But among the men of some intellectual stature who read him, do you believe two out of a hundred take his doctrines seriously and not regard them as a more or less involuntary monomania by which he has allowed himself to be overcome? I have even recently been assured that men interested in his success have very seriously urged him to put aside all this revolutionary trapping, so that the influence they would like to see his journal acquire not be weakened. Does that not prove that for Russia Herzen's journal represents something completely different from the doctrines professed by the editor? Now how can we overlook the fact that what gives it its strength and that to which it owes its success is that for us it represents free discussion, in bad conditions, it is true, in conditions of hatred and bias, but nevertheless free enough— why deny it—to permit the competition of other more reflective, more moderate, and even some positively reasonable opinions. Now that we are certain of where the secret of his strength and influence is, we will have no trouble about the kind of arms we should use to fight him. It is obvious that a journal which would consent to a mission of this kind would have a chance of success only in conditions of existence somewhat analogous to those of its adversary. It is up to you, my Prince, to decide, in your benevolent wisdom, if in the given situation—and you know it better than I— similar conditions are realizable, and up to what point they are so. Assuredly, neither talents, nor zeal, nor sincere convictions would be lacking for this publication; but in hastening

---

[44] *Kolokol* (*The Bell*), which Herzen began publishing in London in 1857. It was by far the most important and influential of the Russian liberal publications and was indeed widely read inside Russia.

to the call addressed to them, they would like, first of all, to be certain that they are participating not in a work of the police, but in a work of conscience; and that is why they would believe themselves right to demand the full measure of liberty a really serious and effective discussion implies and necessitates.[45]

Find out, my Prince, if the influential persons who would superintend the establishment of this journal and protect its existence would agree to assure it the measure of liberty it would need, if perhaps they may not be convinced, through gratitude for the patronage that would be accorded it and through respect for its privileged position, that the journal they might consider in part theirs might not be more guarded and more discreet than all the other journals of the country.

But this letter is too long and I am in haste to finish it. Only allow me, my Prince, in conclusion to add a few words to summarize my entire thought. The project you have had the goodness to communicate to me would appear to me to be of a possible, if not easy, realization, if all opinions, all honest and enlightened convictions have the right openly and freely to establish themselves as an intelligent and de-voted militia under the personal inspiration of the Emperor.

---

[45] Needless to say, the proposed journal was never established.

INDEXES

Each of the entries in this index is followed by the dates of: (1) writing, where available (this date appears in italics); and (2) publication. Although some of the dates of writing are problematic, in no case could the poem have been written after the date given. The reader who wishes further information on the matter of dating is referred to the notes to the Pigarev edition used for this translation. All of the poems except those given the publication dates of 1854, 1868, 1886, 1900, 1913, 1933–34, 1939, and 1957 (years of publication of collections of Tyutchev's poems) first appeared in journals. A list of these journals may be found in the Pigarev edition referred to (pp. 334–36 of vol. 1, and pp. 323–24 of vol. 2). Entries are in both English and transliterated Russian for greater ease of reference.

O, nye tryevozh' menya ukoroi spravyedlivoi (O do not trouble me with just reproach), *1851–52* 1854, 86

O then it was I knew her (Ya znal yeyo yeshcho togda), *1861*, 1868, 102

O this South! O this Nice! (O, etot Yug, o, eta Nitstsa!), *1864*, 1865, 106

O will you long remain concealed (Ty dolgo l' budesh' za tumanom), *1866*, 1868, 143

O vyeshchaya dusha moya (O you, prophetic soul of mine), *1855*, 1857, 93

O you, prophetic soul of mine (O vyeshchaya dusha moya), *1855*, 1857, 93

Obveyan vyeshcheyu dremotoi (Fanned by prophetic dreams), *1850*, 1854, 79

Of that life of yours which once stormed here (Ot zhizni toi, shto bushyevala zdyes'), *1871*, 1886, 119

Oft have you heard me vow (Nye raz ty slyshala priznan'ye), *1851*, 1932, 83

Oleg's Shield (Olyegov shchit), *1829*, 1829, 124

Olyegov shchit (Oleg's Shield), *1829*, 1829, 124

On Reading the Dispatches of the Imperial Cabinet, Printed in the "Journal de St. Petersburg" (Po prochtyenii dyepesh imperatorskovo kabinyeta, napechatannykh v "Journal de St.-Pétersbourg"), *1867*, 1868, 150

On Sending the New Testament (Pri posylkye novoyu zavyeta), *1861*, 1861, 103

On the Eve of the First Anniversary of August 4, 1864 (Nakanunye godovshchiny 4

avgusta 1864), *1865*, 1903, 110

On the Jubilee of Prince Peter Andreyevich Vyazemsky (Na yubilei knyazya Pyotr Andreyevicha Vyazemskovo), *1861*, 1861, 101

On the Neva (Na Nyeva), *1850*, 1854, 77

On the Occasion of the Coming of the Austrian Archduke to the Burial of Nicholas (Po sluchayu priyezda avstriiskovo ertsgertsova na pokhorny imperatora Nikolaya), *1855*, 1868, 138

On the Occasion of Goethe's Death (Na dryeve chelovyechestva vysokom), 1879, 44

On the Way Back (Na vozratnom puti), *1859*, 1860, 98

Ona sidyela na polyu (She was sitting on the floor), *1858*, 1858, 96

Opyat' stoyu Ya nad Nyevoi (Again I stand before the Neva), *1868*, 1903, 113

Osyennei pozdnyeyu poroyu (I love the garden of Tsarskoe Selo), *1858*, 1859, 97

Osyennei vyecher (Autumn Evening), *1830*, 1840, 40

Ot zhizni toi, shto bushyevala zdyes' (Of that life of yours which once stormed here), *1871*, 1886, 119

Our Century (Nash vyek), *1851*, 1851, 83

Pamyati V. A. Zhukovskovo (In Memory of V. A. Zhukovsky), *1852*, 1854, 89

Peace (Uspokoyeniye), *1858*, 1858, 97

Plamya rdyeyet, plamya pyshyet (The flame glows red, the flame flares up), *1855*, 1885, 92

Play on, while over you (Igrai,

n.26; question of, 168; replacement of, 12; Rome destroyer of, 21; Slavic, 11, 19; system of, 180; Tyutchev as preserver of, 18
Universal Gazette. See Augsburg Universal Gazette
Universe, 11, 13, 14, 15, 21

Vatican, 188 n.35
Veneration, religious, 198
Verse, musical quality of Tyutchev's, 14
Vestnik Evropy, 9 n.19
Vienna, 182, 186
Violence, unbridled, 179
Void, intellectual, 206
Volk, 18
Vyazemsky, Prince P. A., 6, 7

War, 194; Franco-Prussian, 15, 20; Thirty Years', 163
Wars, Napoleonic, 16
Weimar, Russian minister at, 6
West: Christian destinies of, 204;

Church of, 192; developments in, 6; disasters for, 166; European, 164, 165, 167; ideas of, 191; last religion of, 189; onslaughts of, 19; peoples of, 173; rationalists of, 22; religious conscience of, 197; revolutionary, 12; royalties of, 187; scholars of, 193; split of, 188; struggle agitating, 190
Westerners, 11, 189
Wholeness, Slavic, 18
World: Catholic, 197; fashioning of, 166; God's, 14; kingdom of this, 191; natural, 15; official, 208; scepter of, 199
Wrath, national, 170

Yaroslavl, 5

Zhukovsky, Vasili Andreyevich, 7
Zosima, Father (Dostoevsky's character), 14